THE EUROPEAN HISTORY SERIES

SERIES EDITOR

KEITH EUBANK

ARTHUR S. LINK
GENERAL EDITOR FOR HISTORY

IN THE WAKE
OF COLUMBUS

THE IMPACT OF THE
NEW WORLD ON EUROPE
1492–1650

ROGER SCHLESINGER

WASHINGTON STATE UNIVERSITY

HARLAN DAVIDSON, INC.

WHEELING, ILLINOIS 60090-6000

Copyright © 1996

Harlan Davidson, Inc.

All Rights Reserved

Library of Congress Cataloging-in-Publication Data

Schlesinger, Roger, 1943–

In the wake of Columbus : the impact of the New World on Europe,

1492–1650 / Roger Schlesinger.

p. cm. — (The European history series)

Includes bibliographical references and index.

ISBN 0-88295-917-4

1. Europe—Civilization—16th century. 2. Europe—

Civilization—17th century. 3. Culture diffusion—Europe—

History—16th century. 4. Culture diffusion—Europe—History—17th

century. 5. Europe—Colonies—America. 6. Europe—Relations—

America. 7. America—Relations—Europe. I. Title. II. Series:

European history series (Wheeling, Ill.)

CB401.S34   1996

940.2—dc20   95-47622

CIP

Cover credit: Four portraits of inhabitants of the "New World," from *Les vrais pourtraits et vies des hommes illustres*, by André Thevet. Courtesy of the Edward E. Ayer Collection, The Newberry Library.

Manufactured in the United States of America

99 98 97 96 1 2 3 4 5 TS

FOR MARY

FOREWORD

Now more than ever there is a need for books dealing with significant themes in European history, books offering fresh interpretations of events which continue to affect Europe and the world. The end of the Cold War has changed Europe, and to understand the changes, a knowledge of European history is vital. Although there is no shortage of newspaper stories and television reports about politics and life in Europe today, there is a need for interpretation of these developments as well as background information that neither television nor newspapers can provide. At the same time, scholarly interpretations of European history itself are changing.

A guide to understanding Europe begins with knowledge of its history. To understand European history is also to better understand much of the American past because many of America's deepest roots are in Europe. And in these days of increasingly global economic activity, more American men and women journey to Europe for business as well as personal travel. In both respects, knowledge of European history can deepen one's understanding, experience, and effectiveness.

The European History Series introduces readers to the excitement of European history through concise books about the great events, issues, and personalities of Europe's past. Here are accounts of the powerful political and religious movements which shaped European life in the past and which have influenced events in Europe today. Colorful stories of rogues and heroines, tyrants, rebels, fanatics, generals, statesmen, kings, queens, emperors, and ordinary people are contained in these concise studies of major themes and problems in European history.

Each volume in the series examines an issue, event, or era which posed a problem of interpretation for historians. The chosen topics are neither obscure nor narrow. These books are neither historiographical essays, nor substitutes for textbooks, nor monographs with endless numbers of footnotes. Much thought and care have been given to their writing style to avoid academic jargon and overspecialized focus. Authors of the European History Series have been selected not only for their recognized scholarship but also for their ability to write for the general reader. Using primary and secondary sources in their writing, these authors bring alive the great moments in European history rather than simply cram factual material into the pages of their books. The authors combine more in-depth interpretation than is found in the usual survey accounts with synthesis of the finest scholarly works, but, above all, they seek to write absorbing historical narrative.

Each volume contains a bibliographical essay which introduces readers to the most significant works dealing with their subject. These are works that are generally available in American public and college libraries. It is hoped that the bibliographical essays will enable readers to follow their interests in further reading about particular pieces of the fascinating European past described in this series.

Keith Eubank
Series Editor

CONTENTS

i x

ACKNOWLEDGMENTS

I want to express thanks to several individuals who assisted me with this project: Jacqueline Wick and Laurie Mercier for typing and research at the beginning; Robert Hadlow for reading the final draft and improving upon it; Richard Hume (former Chair of the History Department at Washington State University) for encouragement and some financial support; Mary Watrous for her intelligent suggestions about the form and content of this book; and Maureen Hewitt for improving, clarifying, and enriching my prose.

INTRODUCTION

About five hundred years ago Christopher Columbus "discovered" America and changed the history of the world. The recent celebration of the quincentennial anniversary of his first voyage has stimulated historians and other scholars to reexamine the impact of his achievement. These reassessments have focused primarily on the changes, for better or worse, that Europeans advanced in the Americas. The encounter of these two worlds, however, also brought considerable changes to European civilization, and those changes are the subject of this book.

Any attempt to assess the impact of the exploration and conquest of America on early modern Europe must consider several different subjects, because the existence of America influenced the development of European civilization in a variety of ways. The European encounter with America had important intellectual consequences: it brought Europeans into contact with new lands and peoples, and in so doing challenged their traditional assumptions about geography, theology, history, and human nature. In addition, America changed Europe's commercial patterns, promising new opportunities for the expansion of European economic activity and an increase in profits. It also introduced a vast array of new products such as potatoes, tobacco, corn, cocoa, chocolate, and sugar into the lives of millions of Europeans. Moreover, the acquisition by European states of lands and resources in America had important political repercussions as well. It affected their diplomatic relations by bringing about changes in the balance of power within Europe, and fostered the growth of overseas rivalries too.

Columbus's encounter with America in 1492 marks one of the great turning points in European, and world, history, symbolizing the beginning of the new relationship between Western Europe and the rest of the world. To fully understand the effect that this "discovery" had on European life, it is necessary to know something about the voyages of exploration themselves.

Half an hour before sunrise on 3 August 1492, Christopher Columbus and his crew of about ninety men sailed from Spain intent on finding a new and shorter route to the riches of Asia. The little fleet of three ships—the *Niña, Pinta,* and *Santa Maria*—stopped first at the Canary Islands, which already belonged to Spain, to restock provisions and to fix the *Pinta's* rudder. On 6 September the expedition left the Canaries, navigating due west. Ten days later the fleet reached the Sargasso Sea, an immense patch of seaweed in the Atlantic. Columbus and his crew concluded that they were near land, and from this point on they eagerly anticipated reaching Asia. Although the ships made good speed across the Atlantic, Columbus deceived his crew by reporting that they had covered less distance (and were therefore closer to Spain) than he really believed they had. In fact, Columbus had computed the circumference of the earth incorrectly, and the "phony" distances that he reported to his crew represented a fairly accurate measurement. Nevertheless, his men eventually started to complain about the length of the voyage and demanded to return home. Columbus persevered, however, and about 2:00 A.M. on 12 October, thirty-three days after leaving the Canaries, he found land. Precisely where this happened is still a matter of considerable debate, but many scholars believe that Columbus made his landfall on the small island of San Salvador in the Bahamas.

Later that morning Columbus went ashore to take possession of the island for Ferdinand and Isabella, the Spanish monarchs whom he served. His *Journal* includes a detailed description of the natives, who appeared friendly and surrounded the ship in their dug-out canoes. From his very first contact with these "Indians," Columbus thought of converting them to Christianity—he did not think that they had any religion of their own. He also observed how submissive and obedient they were. Before long, Spaniards simply expected Native Americans to be their servants, and the natives' unwillingness to serve in this capacity eventually proved fatal.

The gold ornaments that some of the natives wore around their necks attracted Columbus and his crew to the point of obsession. The north-central portion of Hispaniola, another island in the Caribbean, contained a modest source of gold. In the course of his first expedition, Columbus came close to this area and collected some gold ornaments by trading with the natives. The very existence of this gold convinced Columbus that Asia, with its huge deposits of gold, lay close by. Now Columbus began his search for it, destroying the economic structure and social organization of the Caribbean natives in the process.

After encountering several small Caribbean islands and the northern coast of Cuba, Columbus lost his flagship, the *Santa Maria*, which ran aground on a reef off Hispaniola on 24 December and had to be abandoned. This loss endangered the entire expedition because the *Pinta*, under Captain Martin Pinzón, had ignored Columbus's orders and had left the fleet to sail off alone in search of gold only a few days before. The destruction of the *Santa Maria* meant that Columbus had no choice but to leave about forty of his crew behind in a wooden fort constructed from the wreckage of this ship. The rest of the crew crowded onto the *Niña* for the journey home. The settlement received the name *Navidad* ("Christmas") because of the time of year. After Columbus left Hispaniola on the *Niña* and met up with Pinzón and the *Pinta*, both ships headed for Europe on 16 January 1493. Columbus and Pinzón became separated by a severe storm on the return voyage, and later a second storm forced Columbus to land in Portugal rather than Spain. In Lisbon, the Portuguese king received him graciously, and Columbus showed the king Native Americans whom he had kidnapped in the Caribbean. He then continued on to Spain, while Portuguese negotiators began to discuss the ramifications of Columbus's expedition with the Spaniards.

Upon his arrival in Spain, Columbus sent an account of his expedition to Ferdinand and Isabella. This letter shows that Columbus believed that he had reached Asia, and that Cuba formed a part of the Asian mainland. He emphasized the wealth of the "Indies"—especially the gold. From this letter, it appears that Columbus never considered the peoples that he had encountered as anything but inferior to Europeans. As could be expected, the results of the voyage delighted Ferdinand and Isabella, who then honored Columbus at the royal court and approved his proposals for another voyage. At the same time, the Spanish government began negotiations with the pope to secure a monopoly in the lands that Columbus had found.

Pope Alexander VI, a Spaniard himself, proved cooperative. He issued a series of edicts granting Spain control over all lands that Columbus had found—or would find—on subsequent expeditions. Alexander also defined the Spanish and Portuguese spheres of influence by drawing an imaginary line running north to south about one hundred leagues west of the Cape Verde Islands: everything west of the line belonged to Spain. Finally, the pope simply canceled all other rights of discovery and possessions given previously to other European nations.

Portugal, of course, felt itself threatened by Alexander's decisions in these matters, and the Portuguese king, John II, used all of his influence to challenge the pope's favorable treatment of Spanish claims to newly encountered lands. Direct negotiations between Spain and Portugal resulted in the Treaty of Tordesillas in 1494. It moved the papal line of demarcation 270 leagues to the west, leaving intact Portuguese claims to the entire eastern route to Asia and, later, to Brazil.

Before the treaty was finished, Columbus had returned to the Caribbean. He had left Spain in September 1493 with a fleet of seventeen ships carrying a combined crew of about fifteen hundred men. In addition to sailors, these included soldiers, farmers, and craftsmen, together with the necessary equipment for farming and building settlements. Clearly he intended this second expedition to colonize Hispaniola—to build a self-sufficient base from which to conduct further explorations. This fleet made a swift passage across the Atlantic, but found on arrival in Hispaniola that the earlier settlement, with its forty men, had been wiped out. Columbus established a new settlement, which he called Isabella, then set out to find China (he found the south coast of Cuba and Jamaica instead). On his return to Isabella he found that Spaniards and natives were at war with each other. Spanish demands for the natives' gold and food and for native women had infuriated these people. Before Columbus's arrival, gold had played only a small part in Native Americans' economic life, and they now lacked both the skill and desire to satisfy the Europeans' lust for the precious metal. Spaniards retaliated with brutality and enslavement—they killed thousands of Native Americans and shipped hundreds of others to Spain where they quickly died.

In 1496 Columbus put his brother Bartholomew in charge of the settlement and returned to Spain to answer questions about his administration of the colony. Now he needed a successful expedition to prove conclusively that he had reached Asia. Although Ferdinand and Isabella were growing increasingly dubious about Columbus's abilities as an administrator, they agreed to support yet another expedition. This time he sailed to the south of his previous routes, exploring Trinidad and the northern shore of the Gulf of Paria, on the South American mainland. From Paria, Columbus crossed the Caribbean to Santo Domingo, built under the authority of Bartholomew, only to find that some of the settlers had rebelled against his brother. In order to appease the settlers, and to compensate them for the lack of gold, Columbus started to grant parcels of land to individual Spaniards. These soon came to include not only the ownership of a certain piece of real estate, but also of all Native Americans living on it. Thus, the native people found themselves under the authority of their new master, who remained free to exploit them as he wished. This was the birth of the *encomienda* system which later spread to Mexico and Peru and became the basis of Spanish rule in the Americas.

Unfortunately, new grants of land did not substantially improve the spirit of the settlers, or their relationship with the Columbus brothers. Spaniards who returned to Spain complained to the government about the brothers' oppressive administration and described to Queen Isabella the bad treatment that Native Americans were receiving at the hands of her Spanish subjects. Disturbed by these reports, Ferdinand and Isabella appointed Francisco de Bobadilla to replace Columbus in 1499 and to investigate the complaints against him. Bobadilla acted vigorously, sending Columbus home in chains. Although Isabella released him from custody upon his arrival in Spain and restored his property rights, she prohibited Columbus from ever setting foot in Hispaniola again.

Ferdinand and Isabella eventually decided to give Columbus a final opportunity to find a western route to Asia, however, because they still hoped to beat the Portuguese to the source of the spices that Europeans coveted so much. In 1502, Columbus set out on his fourth, and last, voyage to seek a way through the islands that seemed to block the route to the Asian mainland. Lasting about two and a half years, longer than any other, this voyage allowed Columbus to explore the Atlantic coast of Central America. Unexpected storms, fierce fighting with Native Americans, and a mutiny by his crew made this expedition a disaster. Back in Spain, Columbus faced an unenthusiastic royal couple. When Isabella, his strongest supporter, died in 1504, Columbus's career as an explorer died with her. Columbus himself lived for only two more years. His reputation and honor were maintained by his sons Ferdinand, who wrote a biography of his father, and Diego, who became governor of Hispaniola.

By the time that Bobadilla sent Columbus to Spain in chains, other explorers began to expand the search for a westward route to Asia. In 1499, Juan de la Cosa, Alonso de Hojeda (who had sailed with Columbus earlier), and Amerigo Vespucci explored the coast of Venezuela. De la Cosa eventually became famous for a map of the world that he drew around 1500. It provides a good example of how Europeans pictured the world at that date. The map shows a continuous coastline from northeastern Canada to Brazil, but with a gap where Panama is located. Perhaps this is where the passage to Asia existed—de la Cosa left that question unanswered: he covered the area with a picture of St. Christopher.

Eventually the Italian Amerigo Vespucci became even better known than de la Cosa. In addition to his voyage in 1499, he also explored the South American coast for the Portuguese in 1501. During his lifetime, he achieved a good deal of fame because of his detailed written accounts of his explorations. Precisely because Vespucci excelled at public relations and self-promotion, he gained the fame that Spaniards thought Columbus deserved. Martin Waldseemüller, a German mapmaker who relied on the accounts attributed to Vespucci (at least some of them appear to have been forgeries), suggested that the new lands should be named after him—and he used a Latin version of his first name, "America," to designate them on his 1507 map of the region. To this day it is not clear whether Vespucci realized that he had explored the coastline of a new continent or thought it was a long peninsula stretching southward out of China.

Exactly when Europeans realized that the Americas constituted a huge land mass about which they previously had known nothing is hard to say, but most scholars associate that perception with the voyage of the Portuguese explorer Ferdinand Magellan. After leaving Portuguese service because of a dispute with the king over an increase in his salary, Magellan entered the service of the Spanish king Charles I (soon to be Holy Roman Emperor Charles V). In September 1519, Magellan set out to find the elusive westward route to Asia. Historians know a good deal about his voyage through the journal written by a member of the expedition, Antonio Pigafetta. Magellan's fleet of five ships sailed down the west coast of Africa, then crossed the Atlantic to Rio de Janeiro. After putting down a serious mutiny, Magellan continued down the east coast of South America and through what became known as the Strait of Magellan at the southern tip. The passage through the strait, which still is one of the most difficult in the world to navigate, took thirty-eight days. Indeed, one of Magellan's ships turned around and went home. By November 1520, the three remaining ships entered the Pacific Ocean, where more trials and tribulations waited (Magellan was killed by natives in the Philippines). In the end, one ship, commanded by Juan el Cano, with only nineteen survivors, reached Seville on 6 September 1522, more than three years after their departure. Magellan's circumnavigation of the world, of course, demonstrated amazing feats of navigation, endurance, and courage, but the contribution to geography turned out to be even more important. After 1522, few could doubt that America and Asia were two distinctly different regions, separated by a huge ocean previously unknown to Europeans.

From the vantage point of the late twentieth century, it appears quite clear that Columbus, by bringing European civilization into contact with the Americas, began a series of changes in world history that, in the long run, have proven to be of truly monumental proportions. Thanks to Columbus, European society expanded beyond the confines of the European continent itself and eventually reached a degree of world domination without parallel. Over the next few centuries, Europeans imposed their values, institutions, and technology on virtually every foreign society with which they came into contact.

Although it is obvious in retrospect that Columbus and the Renaissance explorers who followed in his wake began a process that dramatically changed the history of the world, the extent to which Renaissance Europeans were aware of these profound changes remains uncertain. While knowledge about new lands, new peoples, and a vast new ocean aroused excitement and stimulated controversy, Europeans remained essentially inward-looking. Events elsewhere were of secondary importance.

At first glance, it may seem indisputable that Renaissance explorations must have exercised a profound and varied impact on European society. Yet, some historians have argued persuasively that the effect on Europe of Columbus's encounter with America has been exaggerated. The British historian, John Elliott, for example, provided a good summary of the debate in the opening chapter of *The Old World and the New*, a book which first appeared in 1970. Elliott argued that, at a certain point, Europeans simply were overwhelmed with all of the new information coming from America. "Mental shutters" came down, and Europeans simply ignored the American challenge to their traditional values and beliefs when it became too great and too bizarre. Since 1970, many historians have come to agree with Elliott's position that the influence of America on European life was "blunted" and that European ideas about their own superiority interfered with any true appreciation of America and its inhabitants.

Whether Europeans really understood what was happening or not, however, the fact remains that European contacts with America began to change European civilization almost from the moment that Columbus returned from his first voyage, and certainly these changes were well underway by the middle of the sixteenth century. The important question, therefore, is not *whether* European society changed, but *how* it changed. In some areas of society, of course, change was greater than in others, and in some cases American influences tell only a part of the story. This book focuses on some of the basic elements of Renaissance society—economics, politics, thought, and daily life—to assess the influences of America on European civilization. In the process, this brief study examines many of the most important, intriguing, and sometimes startling ways in which Europe's relationship with America changed European life in the century or so after Columbus's expeditions.

1 / EUROPEAN ECONOMICS AND AMERICA

The discovery of America, the rounding of the Cape, opened up fresh ground for the rising bourgeoisie. The East-Indian and Chinese markets, the colonization of America, trade with the colonies, the increase in the means of exchange and in commodities generally, gave to commerce, to navigation, to industry, an impulse never before known, and thereby, to the revolutionary element in a tottering feudal society, a rapid development.

KARL MARX
The Communist Manifesto (1848)

Economic trends in Renaissance Europe provide an excellent example of the difficulties involved in evaluating the impact of the exploration and conquest of America on European life. Beginning in the sixteenth century, Europe experienced an unprecedented period of high inflation that had such drastic, and dire, effects on peoples' lives that it has become known as the "Price Revolution." At about the same time, enormous amounts of gold and silver from the rich mines of Central and South America flowed into European markets. Sixteenth-century intellectuals, searching for the cause of the unsettling rise in prices, blamed the influx of American precious metals. Although the connection appeared logical to Renaissance thinkers, modern historians believe that their explanation was incorrect. What, then, is the connection between the so-called Price Revolution and the influx of American gold and silver into the European economy? How did the encounter with America affect European economic life in general? The answers to these questions help to define the role that the "New World" played in European history; they also illuminate some of the ways in which modern historians interpret the events of the past.

Although precise data for the sixteenth century are scarce, it appears that during the Price Revolution the price of wheat, the basic food of the time, increased by about 425 percent in England, 318 percent in the Netherlands, 651 percent in France, 271 percent in Austria, and 376 percent in Castile. Even when prices of manufactured goods, which rose more slowly, are taken into account, the picture is clear: by the middle of the sixteenth century, fast-rising prices had become a fact of life everywhere in Western Europe. At the start of the seventeenth century, wholesale grain prices in England stood about five times higher than they had been toward the end of the sixteenth century. In France, they had risen by more than seven times, and even more than that in southern Spain. People suffered throughout Europe when the price of bread and other staples increased at these levels.

Workers' wages simply failed to keep pace with the rising prices. Everywhere the available evidence tells the same story. In parts of England, Spain, and Austria, workers in the construction industry saw their purchasing power decline by more than 50 percent in the sixteenth century. In the German city of Speyer, during the century after 1520, wages more than doubled; but in the same period, the cost of basic foods skyrocketed. In 1620, rye cost fifteen times more than it had a century earlier, and there were similar rises in the prices of wheat and peas. Meat and salt cost six times more in 1620 than in 1520. In the French city of Poitou, a farmhand's wages in 1578 purchased only 52 percent of what they would have bought in 1470 and the income of a mower had declined to 58 percent of its former value. Because of inflation in Sicily, consumption of meat by rural people decreased from approximately forty pounds per person per year during the 1400s to only about fifteen pounds per person per year in the 1590s. In all European countries, expensive produce combined with low wages severely affected all sections of the working class.

In some cases, members of the upper class also suffered. By the early sixteenth century, landlords, who eagerly wanted cash to purchase manufactured goods, allowed peasants to give them payments in money, rather than in labor or agricultural produce. Once these new relationships had been established, peasants wanted to continue paying with the devalued cash. Consider the plight of a sixteenth-century noble whose ancestors had imposed a money rent on their peasants. Within a few decades, prices of basic commodities doubled or tripled. What had been an ample cash income quickly became inadequate to meet the demands of upper-class living.

More fortunate nobles still received payments in the form of agricultural produce, and they had an income in goods whose value rose along with inflation. Less fortunate nobles, however, did not simply accept their bad luck, they worked to change the system. In England, for example, the rise in wool prices spurred an "enclosure movement," in which nobles literally put fences around (enclosed) common land that had been used by the peasants for pasturing their livestock. Lords used this enclosed land to feed their sheep, whose wool brought much-needed cash with relatively low overhead (a few shepherds who earned low wages). Socially conscious preachers regularly denounced "sheep eating men" but to no avail. Landlords also tried to change the peasants' leases to their land—from longer to shorter terms—so that they could raise rents more frequently as prices of commodities continued to rise.

Those aristocrats on fixed incomes suffered, too. Significant segments of the nobility saw their purchasing power, and their political strength, crumble. Those in more flexible positions took advantage of the economy and mounted a growing challenge to the old ruling elite. Merchants, bankers, and lawyers with rising cash incomes adjusted more easily and frequently to the changing economic conditions—and they prospered. These groups used some of their newfound wealth to acquire real estate and the influential positions in society that accompanied landowning. In turn, they naturally expected a louder voice in government. Across much of Western Europe, there existed a "crisis of the aristocracy," as new forces challenged the traditional ruling elite.

Without doubt, the Price Revolution and the defensive policies of the upper class contributed to two of the most disturbing problems of the sixteenth century: pauperism and vagrancy. Beggars, vagabonds, and criminals became much more visible. In 1531, the English Parliament enacted legislation providing that beggars and vagabonds should be whipped and encouraged to go elsewhere, preferably to the town or village where they were born. Governments condemned begging as both a national calamity and a social nuisance. Over the next half century, Parliament passed several laws designed either to punish or to provide for the poor. Obviously, the problem had become so severe that it attracted the government's attention.

In addition to the tensions caused in agriculture by the rise in prices, problems between employers and employees aggravated other sectors of the economy. Workers tried to get better terms from their bosses; they agitated for higher wages. In some places strikes occurred, and in others workers organized riots. These labor troubles became so severe that both the French and English governments took legal steps to suppress them by prohibiting strikes and regulating wages.

Although few sixteenth-century Europeans could explain why, most recognized that important economic changes were taking place. Some people gained great fortunes while others found themselves in dire economic straits. At first, intellectuals and preachers blamed inflation on the greedy and selfish behavior of speculators and moneylenders, and on the debasement of the coinage (decreasing the silver content). By the middle of the sixteenth century, however, European intellectuals began to associate inflation with the huge amounts of American gold and silver coming into the European economy. Although some professors at the University of Salamanca were the first to make this connection, the Frenchman Jean Bodin (d. 1596) gave it intellectual respectability. He asserted that inflation resulted from an increase in the amount of money in circulation without a comparable increase in the supply of goods. As more and more money chased a stable quantity of goods, he reasoned, the prices of those goods simply had to go up. In France, his ideas found a good deal of acceptance, and soon in England and Spain experts repeated his logic in their own writings. His explanation seemed to make good sense, and it certainly appeared to fit the facts.

Before the middle of the sixteenth century, Europe's supply of silver came from mines in what is now Germany, Austria, and the Czech Republic. Much of it ended up in the hands of Venetians and other Italians, who shipped it to the East in exchange for spices, silks, and other luxury products such as cotton and gold. Europe itself produced only small amounts of gold—about one metric ton a year during the thirteenth and early fourteenth centuries, increasing to three or four tons by the late fourteenth century. Europeans obtained most of their gold from Africa, especially the western Sudan and the Gold Coast, now Ghana. Until the second half of the sixteenth century, Europe suffered from great shortages of gold and silver. This situation changed dramatically when Spanish explorers and "conquistadors" found great deposits of gold, and especially silver, in Mexico and South America.

At first, Europeans found small deposits of gold in the Caribbean. Then they found vast amounts of silver in Peru and Mexico. Europeans discovered Potosí, the most important mine in Peru, in 1545, but its efficient exploitation proceeded only after a local supply of mercury to refine the silver was found in Huancavelica (in Peru) in 1563. This produced more than half the mercury needed at Potosí; they imported the rest from Spain. The population of Potosí rose from about 45,000 in 1545 to 120,000 in 1585, and 160,000 in 1610, which gives some idea of the enterprise's size and the amount of labor needed to work the mine.

At its peak, production of silver in all the Americas, including the major Mexican mines at Guanajuato and Zacatecas, reached 300 tons a year. Spanish *encomenderos* used some of it locally and shipped considerable amounts directly to Manila and China in exchange for luxury goods: on the average, they shipped about 170 tons of silver a year to Spain. Spanish merchants, in turn, traded their bullion in Europe for all sorts of manufactured and food products. As a result of these lucky discoveries, Europe's supply of gold and silver more than tripled between 1500 and 1650; Europeans received more gold (181 tons) and silver (16,000 tons) from America between 1500 and 1650 than existed in Europe in 1500. Considering the sudden presence of so much American treasure in Europe, it is easily understood why Europeans identified these precious metals as the cause of their inflation. Furthermore, the inflationary trend seemed to follow the path of the American gold and silver as it moved from Spain to the rest of Europe.

According to the economic theories of the age, governments prized gold and silver as the most valuable forms of wealth, and the Spanish government tried to keep as much of it from leaving the country as possible. Spain passed regulations requiring that all American gold and silver be brought to Seville where the king's government took 20 percent of the total through taxation. Despite these measures, however, the economic policy of the Spanish government failed, and other European countries benefitted from the American gold and silver that the Spaniards had found. Throughout the sixteenth century, the Spanish government engaged in wars with many of its neighbors in Europe, and gold and silver flowed out of Spain to pay for this aggressive, and expensive, foreign policy. Government officials spent the treasure as fast, and sometimes faster, than they obtained it. With American treasure as collateral, Spanish monarchs borrowed heavily from German and Italian bankers to equip their fleets, fight their wars, and pay for their trade deficit with the rest of Europe. Silver poured into Seville, but it flowed out like water through a sieve on its way to the Netherlands, England, Germany, and Italy to pay the bills. Within a hundred years of the discovery of America, the Dutch, Germans, and northern Italians controlled Spain's colonial trade, and made a handsome profit for themselves. In effect, Spain became merely a transfer point between America and northern European bankers and their great commercial companies.

American gold and silver remained in Spain just long enough to inflate the economy, so the argument ran, then it passed to other regions which experienced a similar inflation. Given their perceptions about the movement of gold and silver on the one hand, and prices on the other, it seems reasonable that thoughtful Europeans assumed that there existed a close relationship between the two. But were they right? Modern scholars have made a strong case that these Europeans were simply wrong in their assumptions and conclusions, and that American bullion did not cause the inflationary spiral that plagued Europe at the time.

Although sixteenth-century Europeans were confident that they had correctly figured out the causes of inflation at the time, twentieth-century historians have found some serious flaws in their argument. For example, prices in Spain and elsewhere began to rise some time before the arrival of American gold and silver. In Germany and France, for instance, prices began going up before the end of the fifteenth century. In England, which received only negligible amounts of American bullion in the early sixteenth century, the price level had already doubled by 1550. In Italy, bullion to support Spanish troops stationed there did not arrive in significant quantities until the 1570s, but prices moved sharply higher as early as the 1530s. In Germany and parts of France, also, price levels rose sharply in the late fifteenth century, even before the galleons loaded with bullion reached Spain. In most of Europe, prices rose most steeply before 1565, but bullion imports from America reached their peak between 1580 and 1620. There simply is no direct correlation between bullion imports and the inflation rate, despite what observers at the time thought. Clearly, something besides imports of American gold and silver caused this inflation. A clue to the identity of the root cause lies in the way that prices of different kinds of goods fluctuated.

Studies of these price fluctuations show that grain prices normally increased about twice as much as prices for nonagricultural items, suggesting that the demand for food exceeded that for manufactured goods. Today, historians believe that the demand for food rose faster than production—hence a rise in prices—precisely because the European population itself, literally the number of mouths to feed, increased dramatically. Some of the other inflationary patterns of the time tend to support this interpretation as well. For example, land values increased noticeably, indicating that the growing population needed more real estate. No one, however, knows why the population increased. Opinions vary, but it appears that between about 1450 and 1600—despite war, famine, and plague—Europe witnessed a population increase of some twenty to thirty-five million people (roughly a 50 percent increase). Further escalating the price of food, the urban population, which produced no food, grew most quickly. In 1500, for example, only four European cities contained over 100,000 people, but in 1600, the number of such cities had tripled.

The search for the causes of the Price Revolution shows how modern historians can sometimes understand the fundamental workings of a past society better than the people who lived at the time. In this particular case, the influence of America on Europe had only a subjective reality: sixteenth-century people perceived an influence that turned out to be only an illusion. That is an influence of a kind, but America also had other, more direct, influences on European economic life.

The Price Revolution not only made life more difficult for various segments of the population, it adversely affected the European governments of the period as well. Their activities, especially the waging of war, became much more expensive— while tax revenues dwindled. As a result, governments resorted to "debasing" their coinage (reducing the value of its metallic content), causing a good deal of financial instability. Governments' attempts to raise more money to pay for their various activities also brought them into conflict with important vested interest groups within society. As with the root causes of the inflation, contemporaries tended to place the blame for their troubles on the influx of American silver.

As American silver began to penetrate the European economy, governments used the precious metal in their coins in order to increase their value. In Naples, for example, the government placed some 10.5 million ducats in circulation between 1548 and 1587. Yet, by the latter date, only 700,000 remained in circulation. The rest had fallen into the hands of speculators and hoarders who believed their value would rise because of their silver content. In France, inflation of the silver coinage led the government to attempt to limit the face value of the coins (in 1602). As coins began to disappear from circulation, the French treasury replaced them with debased coinage. Also, foreigners enjoyed this speculation: a report from Lyons in 1601 had claimed that German and Swiss traders in the city were hoarding coins to carry out of the country.

Spain, the source of the silver, suffered the most. Hit hard by inflation and budget deficits, the Spanish government declared bankruptcy with amazing regularity: in 1557, 1575, 1596,

1607, 1627, and 1647. Even as early as 1557 the collapse of Spanish credit brought declarations of bankruptcy from other governments dependent on Spanish silver: France, the Netherlands, Naples, and Milan. In 1599, the Spanish government, trying to find a way out of its financial difficulties, replaced the silver in its coins with copper bought in Europe, and in 1602 it even ordered a reduction in size of its copper coins to save money. Indeed, by 1650 over 98 percent of all Spanish coins contained copper rather than silver.

The same thing happened elsewhere. As private individuals collected more and more silver, governments had less and less of it. After Spain, Europe's chief supplier and importer of silver, ran so short of the metal that the government began issuing copper coins in 1599, similar hoarding of the silver coins, inflation, and budget deficits drove other governments to the same expedient. Spain's government suffered especially severely because it had to finance the military and administrative costs of the largest empire in Europe. An official memorandum of April 1574 earlier illustrated the magnitude of the problem. It estimated that the government's income for the coming year would be about 5.5 million ducats, of which it could expect only 1 million from America in the form of silver bullion. At that time, however, the government's total debt amounted to over 73 million ducats (over 4 million ducats were owed to the Netherlands alone). Other estimates made at the same time differ slightly, but the ratio between income and debt remained about the same.

Since the real value of taxes also declined because of inflation, governments searched for new ways to meet their financial obligations. In their hunt for more money, they clashed with wealthy segments of the society that had traditionally been exempt from taxation. Opposition to new governmental tax schemes sparked several revolutions that occurred throughout Europe in the 1640s. Those who favored increasing the power of the government to raise taxes defended the so-called absolute rights of the crown. The struggle over absolutism, which occupied much of the seventeenth century, consisted primarily of a contest over the rights of governments to raise money. Moreover, in determining the cause of these revolutions, historians learned something about the impact of government policy on taxpayers. In parts of Spain, the level of indirect taxation doubled between 1556 and 1584, outpacing the price rise, and in many regions of France taxes, which had doubled between 1550 and 1580, quadrupled by 1640. Incomes rose but not enough to offset peoples' impression that they were being crippled by rising taxes.

The Price Revolution also stimulated the growth of industrial capitalism because prices increased much faster than wages (except in Spain, where labor remained in short supply). Consequently, owners of industries who purchased cheaper raw materials and converted them to manufactured goods realized large rewards. The resulting increase in profits—or "profit inflation"—gave merchants and industrialists more capital to invest in large-scale enterprises. Many of these new ventures took advantage of European expansion into North and South America, which increasingly were seen as offering good opportunities for making money.

New global markets, enormous supplies of cheap raw materials, and the greater availability of investment capital fundamentally transformed the way Europeans did business. Collectively these changes are usually called the "Commercial Revolution." In reality, they were a series of gradual changes over several centuries that, in the long run, affected virtually every aspect of European life. The Commercial Revolution depended, to a large extent, on European colonies in the Americas.

It is no coincidence that one of the most important effects of the Commercial Revolution—perhaps the most important one—concerned a change in the location of the main centers of European economic activity in the sixteenth century. The growing Portuguese and Spanish dominance of world commerce shifted the center of the trade in Oriental luxury goods from the Mediterranean to the Atlantic. The Italian city-states, which had controlled this trade in Europe, had much less to do with the new and increasingly important trade between Europe and the Americas. Since Spain failed to develop its commercial economy, the region bordering on the North Sea and the English Channel—the Netherlands, England, and northern France—benefitted the most. Entrepreneurs in colonizing nations invested money in overseas exploration and colonial expansion. Here, merchants organized and supplied expeditions for trade with the rest of the world. Colonial goods from the far corners of the earth found markets in these countries, which incidently, had the advantage of possessing the best ports in Europe, conveniently located for using the new routes across the Atlantic and around Africa to the Indies.

Under these circumstances, not surprisingly, cities like Cadiz, Lisbon, Bordeaux, Rouen, Antwerp, Amsterdam, Bristol, and London grew increasingly large and important in the decades following the European exploration and conquest of America. Ships crowded Lisbon's port, on the Tagus River, in the 1540s; Antwerp, at its commercial peak in the 1560s, saw some five hundred ships a day pass up and down the Scheldt River; in the period between 1588 and 1618 the number of English ships doubled; and in the middle of the seventeenth century, the Dutch merchant marine became four times larger than Italy's, Spain's, and Portugal's combined.

This shift from the Mediterranean to the Atlantic and the North Sea, part of the so-called Commercial Revolution, constitutes one of the most important changes in European history. It meant that for the next three and a half centuries the Atlantic region of Europe would be the leader in economic activity and experience the greatest degree of financial prosperity. Other areas of Europe did not collapse overnight, however. The Mediterranean continued to be a trade center, and considerable commerce continued in that region. Venice, in particular, retained a major role in European trade (and banking) well into the seventeenth century. Other Mediterranean cities such as Barcelona, Marseilles, and Genoa also continued to prosper despite the Commercial Revolution. Nevertheless, it remains clear that the key position of the Mediterranean region in European economic life tended to stagnate compared with the Atlantic and North Sea in the century or two after Columbus.

European expansion stimulated commerce and capitalism, showering businessmen with new opportunities and new obstacles. One of their most crucial problems concerned the necessity of raising large amounts of investment capital for risky business ventures. By their very nature, New World endeavors involved considerably more risk than most enterprises in the past. The ways in which European governments, as well as private investors, responded to these challenges varied from place to place, but in almost every case they demonstrate the ability to adapt to the new circumstances presented by trade with America.

From both the examples of medieval business practices and the dictates of common sense, Renaissance businessmen discovered that capital required for the new commercial enterprises could be secured in two ways: either by bringing capitalists together as active operators in one enterprise, or by bringing them together in undertakings in which they were strictly investors with no managerial responsibilities. In the first instance, the so-called Regulated Company resulted. In such examples as the English Merchant Adventurers, the Eastland Company, the Levant Company, and later the Muscovy Company, merchants obtained monopoly rights from their governments to trade in certain areas, and they pooled their resources to buy or hire ships. They elected officials from among their number, and these entrepreneurs established the guidelines for each commercial venture. The merchants in these companies, however, traded on their own as private individuals. They bought the goods that they wanted to take to foreign markets with their own money, they did their own selling, and they bought foreign products for their customers at home. They shared certain common expenses of the venture proportionately such as costs for insurance, ships and crews, and land transportation. This strategy kept the individual's capital requirements at a minimum and distributed the risk of loss more evenly. The regulated company had its drawbacks because keen competition existed among its members for overseas business. Placing the blame for a failed voyage usually caused resentment and, sometimes, the company's dissolution.

From the beginning of the seventeenth century, therefore, an alternative form of business organization, the Joint-Stock Company, became more common. It combined investors' capital without their active involvement in the enterprise. In these cases, a group of businessmen who wanted to pursue a specific commercial project simply issued shares of stock to the investing public at a specific price. In purchasing these shares of stock at a given price, the investors bought part ownership in a business. If it prospered and its property increased in value, they received a share of the earnings in the form of dividends, computed according to the amount of their original investment. In addition, the value of shares in a successful venture increased, and they also profited by this "appreciation." On the other hand, if the business failed, investors shared the liability for the debts of the company according to the number of shares they owned.

This joint-stock arrangement became one of the most important innovations in business organization in the history of European civilization. Its great advantage and popularity arose because it could tap the savings of a large number of investors, and thus could bring together the large sums required for the newly profitable, but risky, overseas business transactions. Simultaneously, it gave public citizens a way to put surplus capital to work, even in small amounts, without involving them in the complicated and technical tasks of the venture. Of more wide-ranging consequence, it allowed the investors to get cash when they needed it by making the shares negotiable on the open market. The joint-stock organization also had the advantage of surviving the death of any of the individual owners: those who inherited the shares of the deceased owners simply became the new owners, and the business went forward as though nothing had happened. This allowed for long-range planning and continuity of company policy. In time, investors in joint-stock companies even saw their potential losses limited to no more than the amount they had invested.

In the seventeenth century, joint-stock companies were formed first to take advantage of the lucrative trade with Asia. In 1600, for example, the English government granted a royal charter to the East India Company. The charter gave the Company a monopoly of trade in the East Indies, and made it responsible for exercising administrative authority in India and Indochina, where it traded. Indeed, the Company acted as a government in those ports where it controlled the export trade. Two years later, in 1602, the Dutch government chartered its own East India Company to compete with the English. Like its English twin, this organization grew by combining multiple partnerships and regulated companies, which had been created for specific trading voyages to the East. The Dutch Company's charter also gave it a monopoly of trade and the obligation and right to exercise all the privileges and powers usually held by governments (such as the right to seize and defend territory, declare war and make peace, administer justice, and enact local laws) in the areas where it did business. France did not establish a trading company until 1664, when Jean Baptiste Colbert (d. 1613), Louis XIV's minister for economic affairs, convinced a group of private businessmen that France should not leave the lucrative Indies trade to the English and Dutch. His support made the project workable. He gave the organizers of the Company a charter with privileges and powers similar to those of the English and Dutch Companies; and when the French investing public bought only about half of the stock in the Company, Colbert persuaded the king to buy up the rest.

The three great East India companies firmly established the joint-stock company as the best vehicle for colonial trade. It is not surprising, therefore, that joint-stock companies also formed to initiate settlement and trade in the Americas. The Dutch established a West India Company in 1621, and the French followed about a quarter of a century later. The English used the joint-stock approach for their Virginia Company in 1603, Hudson's Bay Company in 1624, and Massachusetts Bay Company in 1630. By the end of the seventeenth century, the joint-stock company had become one of the most important features of European economic and political life. The activities of the East and West India Companies provide a good illustration of the close relationship between economics and politics that existed in seventeenth-century Europe. The activities of these companies also show how European governments pursued their "mercantilist" policies.

MERCANTILISM AND AMERICA

Economic developments during the Age of Exploration gave rise to a cluster of government policies called mercantilism. It grew out of the revival of long-distance trade, the acquisition of colonies by the European powers, and the rise of strong, centralized governments. In addition, mercantilism tried to explain and shape the proper roles of money, commerce, production, and colonies for stimulating the economic growth of a nation.

It also promoted the economic health of society by specifically strengthening the economy of the state, thereby providing for stronger centralized control and military power. In this situation, any improvement in the economic well-being of the individual citizen became a secondary consideration at best. Under the mercantilist system, the government regulated all aspects of economic life to increase the power of those in the elite classes of society. In a sense, mercantilism created nothing new, but as governments grew stronger, they obtained more power to regulate their national economies. Now, states engaged in an extensive amount of control over private economic activity, but the way they did it varied from one place to another.

During this period, Portugal provides the best example of the link between government power and economic policy. With its all-water route to the riches of India, the Portuguese government claimed to have a monopoly of trade with the Indies. Almost immediately, it enacted a series of regulations to keep other Europeans from enjoying the profits from this trade, and it conducted its commercial affairs with the express goal of making and keeping money. The Portuguese measured their profit precisely by the amount of gold and silver that they accumulated, and the nation tried to accumulate as much as possible by a favorable balance of trade (the value of exports less the value of imports).

By its practices during the Age of Exploration, the Portuguese government established certain principles that became basic to the doctrine of mercantilism: that colonies existed primarily to be exploited to the benefit of the colonizing power (the "metropolis"); that the metropolis would have a favorable balance of trade with its colonies; and that national wealth was to be measured by the amount of gold and silver a country had within its borders. The prime goal of mercantilists, therefore, was to collect as much gold and silver as possible. These three principles became even more firmly rooted in the theory of mercantilism by the policies of the Spanish government.

Within this general framework, the policies of the different colonial powers varied to meet the different conditions both at home and abroad. In the Western Hemisphere, Spain developed strict regulations so that it could control trade and reap all of its benefits. It required that all trade pass through specific ports in Spain (Cadiz and later Seville) and in America (Porto Bello and Santa Cruz); that ships in the trade sail in fleets to keep out intruders and inhibit pirates; and that foreigners, Jews, and Moslems be kept out of colonial trade. Although the Spaniards introduced European plants and animals into the Americas, they did relatively little to exploit the wealth of their new possessions, except in the case of silver mining.

Eventually Spanish planters grew sugar and tobacco in large quantities in Cuba, Haiti, and Santo Domingo, sheep in Peru, and indigo and cochineal for dyes in more tropical locales, but economic developments in all these regions suffered from Spanish trade regulations. For example, until the late seventeenth century, goods from Argentina had to be transported over the Andes mountains to Peru and then northwards across Panama and then on to Spain. Even worse, Spain permitted the Philippines to send only one ship a year to Mexico for fear that too much silver would enter the China trade. This limit on shipping not only restricted Spanish commerce in the East, it hurt trade with Mexico. It meant that supplies in the Philippines ran critically low, that space aboard ship was very expensive, and that the transportation of goods was unnecessarily costly. Even in the West Indies and Central America, fleets sailed only twice a year, so that sugar and tobacco piled up, raising the costs and risks of storage and causing seasonal shortages and surpluses in European markets. Nevertheless, Spain's colonists eased this situation by trading with foreign smugglers in order to get rid of their products while obtaining the goods they needed at a lower price than they paid to other Spaniards. New Englanders carried on an active trade with the Spanish West Indies and the Dutch broke the Spanish blockade of their colonies so often that they had a virtual monopoly of the Spanish cocoa trade. When the English obtained a thirty-year *asiento* (contract) in 1713 to furnish slaves to the Spaniards, they gained nothing more than legal permission for and recognition of what they already had been doing illegally. Although Spain had succeeded in collecting large amounts of gold and silver, it failed in preventing its gold and silver from leaking out to other European states.

In the eighteenth century, when Spanish political and military power proved unable to maintain its monopoly over colonial trade, the government loosened its regulations. From 1714, the new Spanish king, grandson of France's Louis XIV, officially relinquished his monopoly on New World trade in exchange for income from new import and export taxes. By about 1740, new regulations allowed individual ships to go to the colonies and to trade at any port. In 1764, a regular semimonthly mail service began between the West Indies and Spain. In 1765, colonial trade opened up to all Spaniards; and in 1778, Spain eliminated the fleet system altogether. These more tolerant policies resulted in a considerable increase in Spanish trade with America.

Like the Portuguese and Spaniards, the Dutch wanted to keep the benefits of trade with the East for themselves alone. That was the primary reason they established the Dutch East India Company, which exercised a monopoly over this trade and had the obligation of defending and administering (and exploiting) the colonial empire. In other areas of the world, the Dutch also used trading companies—the Dutch West India Company, for example—but in these regions the Dutch willingly gave up attempts at monopoly and competed with others as best they could. In the long run, however, the Dutch did not achieve a great deal of success.

The Dutch had no industries in their country to protect or enhance. Their activities in the Americas emphasized gaining colonies for trade with the natives and to establish bases from which to conduct smuggling operations with the colonies of other European powers. The Dutch government, unlike its competitors, levied no customs duties on imports. It carefully avoided any policy that might hinder trade. Dutch people did not emigrate to any of their colonies in large numbers, and they showed relatively little enthusiasm for developing colonial agriculture. Although they cultivated some sugar in their West Indian possessions (especially Curaçao and Brazil), the main activity of the Dutch in the West Indies consisted of trading with Spanish colonists. The Dutch government tried to give a monopoly of trade in the region to the Dutch West India Company, which had some successes between 1621 and 1648, but Dutch commerce better suited the activities of single enterprising individuals rather than a large company. Dutch entrepreneurs alienated foreign powers so much that Holland became embroiled in wars with its competitors. Ultimately, Holland lacked the military muscle to defend itself from attack by England, France, and Portugal. By the eighteenth century, the European colonial powers forced the Dutch out of Brazil, New Amsterdam, and Guiana. The Dutch position of primacy in American trade fell to the English.

Sixteenth-century France had neither routes to the riches of the East nor overseas possessions with vast amounts of gold and silver to be taken from natives. Nevertheless, the French government, at the insistence of King Louis XIV's chief economic advisor, Colbert, took steps to accumulate precious metals through a favorable balance of trade. The French realized fairly early how important American colonies might be to their economy, and the government claimed Louisiana and Canada as a result of exploration and took some of the West Indian islands (Martinique, Guadeloupe, and Haiti) from Spain. From the beginning, the French followed strict mercantilist policies in the Americas. Without great success, they attempted to control and develop their colonies through the activities of monopolistic companies. The French West India Company's monopoly lasted only five years and the Company itself was liquidated by 1674. The Canada Company and its successor, the Company of New France, also experienced difficulties and a very short life. From the latter part of the seventeenth century, France governed its American holdings as royal colonies, with the full support of the state.

The French succeeded in getting some agricultural benefits from their possessions in the West Indies. They grew tobacco in the West Indies in the seventeenth century, and the French islands became famous for their sugar production. Further north, in Canada, a flourishing trade developed in fish, fur, and timber. Like the Netherlands, however, France lost many of its overseas possessions in the eighteenth century: it surrendered Acadia (Nova Scotia) to the English in 1713, and ceded Louisiana to Spain later in the century. In 1763, France lost Canada to England, and later lost Haiti to native freedom fighters. France's economic future was in production, rather than foreign commerce, like the Dutch, or exploitation of colonies, like the Spaniards.

Neither Portugal, Spain, nor the Netherlands emphasized the production of either industrial or agricultural goods in their mercantilist policies. English mercantilism developed differently. Although they recognized the advantages of a favorable balance of trade and the value of colonies, the English lacked—at first— the kinds of trading opportunities afforded the Portuguese and the Dutch, and found no Native Americans from whom they could steal tons of gold and silver. The English, therefore, decided to get rich through use of labor and a favorable balance of trade. Adam Smith, the founding father of modern capitalism, captured the spirit of English mercantilism in 1776 in his book *The Wealth of Nations*, when he wrote that the labor of the workers of every nation supplies it with all the essentials and conveniences of life.

In the seventeenth century, the English continued to stress production as the best route to national prosperity. The government reduced the number of regulations governing economic life and allowed industrialists and investors more freedom. It also created a protective tariff to preserve the English market for English goods. At the same time, however, the English took steps to expand their sphere of economic activity, following the examples of the Portuguese and Dutch. They established overseas trading companies (the East and West India Companies), and they went to war with the Dutch on several occasions to reduce competition from their Protestant rival. They also enacted Navigation Acts in 1651, 1660, 1663, and 1673.

The particulars of the Navigation Acts provide an excellent example of just how far the English government was willing to go to achieve economic superiority over its rivals. They provided that goods produced in America, Asia, or Africa must be brought to England in English ships or in ships of an English colony, captained by Englishmen and staffed by English crews. In addition, the acts required that goods produced in Europe had to be brought to England in English ships or in the ships of the country that produced them. They also ordered that produce from Spanish or Portuguese colonial possessions had to be brought in directly from Portugal or Spain—a direct attack on the Dutch carrying trade. The Navigation Acts imposed heavier customs duties on goods carried to England in foreign ships than in English ones, and listed certain items (sugar, tobacco, cotton, indigo, ginger, dye-wood) which had to be sent from an English colony only to England or to another English colony. They further stipulated that most foreign goods (except wine) imported by English colonies had to be carried in English ships sailing from English ports. Finally, they placed special fees on some goods (like sugar) shipped from one English colony to another. The mercantilist program represented by the Navigation Acts tried to make England nothing less than the center of world trade. The accumulation of gold and silver did not become the objective of England's trade, however. It aimed at getting more goods.

While English colonial policy in America conformed to the same basic mercantilist theories about the value of colonies, it differed from them in two important respects. First, English settlers went to colonies in North America in fairly large numbers as permanent settlers (the population of the thirteen colonies of the future United States was about two million in 1776). Second, the English in North America, themselves, produced many of the goods which they needed, rather than concentrating on products for consumers back home in England. Not only did they consider themselves to be the equals of the English at home, they became, in certain respects, commercial rivals of the English. Thus, when the English tried to preserve their own trading and manufacturing interests, the colonists felt oppressed.

Early in their history, English colonists became very successful in shipbuilding because of the quality of abundant raw materials. They had timbers for masts that were without equal in Europe. Indeed, on the eve of the American Revolution, American colonists built one-third of all ships flying the English flag. Success in shipbuilding led directly to shipping, and American carriers, especially those from New England, built up brisk shipping and fishing businesses. They created a triangular trade by carrying fish and flour to the West Indies to trade for sugar and molasses, which they used to make rum. Then, they either sold the sugar and rum to the English, in return for manufactured goods, or took the sweet produce to Africa where they exchanged it for slaves, whom they took back and sold in the colonies. American shippers also carried tobacco and cotton directly to England and brought back supplies for the colonies.

In all trade, colonial ships had the same rights and privileges as English vessels. American colonial shipping suffered, however, when the English in the West Indies decided that American colonists should not be allowed to go to Spanish or French West Indian islands for sugar and molasses. England's sugar-refining interests exerted their influence in obtaining passage of the Molasses Act of 1733, which levied a heavy tax on all sugar and molasses going to the colonies. They charged and proved that colonial sugar refining and rum making were hurting their business. In a similar way, many infant industries in the colonies were injured by legislation to protect the colonial market for English manufacturers. Consequently, the English Parliament passed legislation prohibiting the exports of woolen products (1699) and hats (1731) from one colony to another; the Iron Act (1750) prevented the manufacture of iron and steel products in America, and other laws prohibited colonists from helping the development of their own industries through subsidies. These restrictive policies, of course, helped bring about the American Revolution. The political independence that the colonists gained, however, was not matched by any economic benefit. Indeed, American commerce suffered after the Revolution precisely because American ships no longer enjoyed the trading rights of English ships.

Although the influx of American gold and silver into Europe is now considered to have aggravated, rather than caused, the sixteenth-century Price Revolution, the exploration and conquest of America resulted in some profound changes in the European economy. Perhaps the most important among these is the shift in the European economic center of gravity away from the Mediterranean to those countries bordering the Atlantic. In addition, the opportunities presented by the Atlantic trade gave rise to new forms of business enterprise, especially the joint-stock company. Finally, the economic possibilities offered by overseas colonies helped in the development of mercantilism in virtually every important country in Western Europe. With hindsight, it is easy to see that Karl Marx was correct in identifying the European exploration and conquest of America as a key in the economic development, not only of the European continent, but of the entire world.

2 / EUROPEAN POLITICS AND AMERICA

> The greatest event since the creation of the world (excluding the incarnation and death of Him who created it) is the discovery of the Indies.
>
> FRANCISCO LÓPEZ DE GÓMARA
> *General History of the Indies* (1552)

European exploration and conquest of America brought great change to political life in Europe. By far the most obvious of these changes is the creation of Europe's first worldwide empires. During the Renaissance, Europe's governments extended their authority overseas to far-off lands, and they fought out their traditional rivalries both at home and in their possessions abroad. Consequently, one must conclude that European imperialism affected many facets of political life—for example, relationships between church and state, between subject and ruler, and among the various countries of Europe as well. Each of these groups and institutions now conducted their relationships within a global, rather than strictly European, setting.

Nevertheless, the precise manner in which the exploration and conquest of America affected European political life often eludes the investigator. Many of the changes that took place had origins or basic causes that preceded Columbus's fateful voyage of 1492. Indeed, some historians have argued that the exploration and conquest of America actually exercised an insignificant influence on the development of European politics, and that most of the major political developments would have occurred even if Europeans had never heard of America in the first place. While it remains very difficult to prove this argument one way or the other, as the sixteenth century wore on, the influence of America on European politics became much more important than it had been at the beginning. At the very least, the expansion of European power into the Americas escalated the competition between Protestants and Catholics, and among nations generally, as politicians fought to control these newfound lands.

As soon as they received the first report about Columbus's 1492 voyage, Ferdinand and Isabella tried to acquire a monopoly of navigation and settlement in the seas and lands that he had explored. They easily secured the help of Pope Alexander VI (Rodrigo Borgia), who needed Spanish support for his attempt to create an Italian principality for his son, Cesare Borgia. In order to get it, Alexander, a Spaniard himself, gave Ferdinand and Isabella what they wanted. In 1493, he issued a series of four papal bulls (official proclamations), each strengthening and extending the provisions of the preceding ones. The first two gave Ferdinand and Isabella authority over all lands discovered, or to be discovered, in the regions explored by Columbus. The third bull, the famous *Inter Caetera*, drew the imaginary boundary line from north to south one hundred leagues west of the Azores and Cape Verde Islands, and provided that the lands and seas beyond the line should be a Spanish sphere of exploration. The fourth bull extended the previous grants to include all islands and mainlands that might be found in sailing or traveling west and south towards India.

This last bull, with its reference to India, alarmed the Portuguese government, which wanted to protect its position in the lucrative spice trade. Although King John II of Portugal used all of the political and diplomatic resources at his disposal, he could not convince the pope to revoke the bulls. As a result, John opened direct negotiations with Ferdinand and Isabella. In an effort to compromise, John accepted *Inter Caetera* as a basis for discussion, but he asked that the boundary line be moved 270 leagues further west to protect Portuguese interests in Africa. Ferdinand and Isabella, believing that Columbus had pioneered a shorter and more efficient route to the riches of Asia, agreed with John's request. The resulting Treaty of Tordesillas (1494) allowed Portugal to keep its monopoly of the route to Asia by way of the Cape of Good Hope and paved the way for its later claims to Brazil. The treaty awarded Spain a free hand in what eventually would become known as America. In addition to its provisions, which at the time must have seemed extremely vague, the Treaty of Tordesillas stands as proof that both Spain and Portugal wanted to avoid any political or military conflict over their claims to other parts of the world. In fact, the treaty succeeded in preventing war between Spain and Portugal, but other events conspired to bring America into the arena of European political and military affairs.

In 1494, the same year that Spain and Portugal negotiated the Treaty of Tordesillas, King Charles VIII of France set his sights on conquering the Kingdom of Naples, in southern Italy. To realize his goal, he invaded the Italian peninsula with what contemporaries described as the largest army in all European history. The disunited, and often feuding, Italian city-states could offer no serious resistance to the French invasion, which resembled a triumphal march more than a military campaign. To counterbalance the growing power and influence of France, however, other European powers—especially Spain, also invaded the Italian peninsula. This situation resulted in a series of wars fought between the ruling Valois family of France and the Hapsburgs, who came to control both Spain and the Holy Roman Empire. These Hapsburg-Valois wars lasted from 1494 to 1559 and turned France and Spain into deadly enemies. Two years after making peace with Portugal, Spain found itself facing French attacks in Europe—and in America.

EUROPEAN RIVALRIES IN AMERICA

By the early sixteenth century France exerted a strong naval presence in the Atlantic both because of the royal navy and because of its seamen who became pirates. It had participated in the proposed conquest of the Canary Islands in 1344, and by the late fifteenth century the French navy presented the most formidable opposition to Spain and Portugal in the Atlantic. Caribbean sugar planters feared French ships that raided Portuguese settlements in Brazil as early as 1504. By 1537, Spaniards complained, with good reason, that French pirates were attacking Spanish ships returning from America. In addition to some three hundred Portuguese ships that had been captured by French pirates in the first three decades of the sixteenth century, a squadron, belonging to the French businessman and shipowner Jean Ango, seized a Spanish ship carrying Aztec treasure home to Spain in 1523. The French pirates' reputation was such that when Spanish seamen sighted any strange ship in the Atlantic, they assumed that it was French—and hostile.

Since the French believed that wealth from America financed Spanish military power in Europe, they increased their attacks on Spanish shipping and settlements in the Caribbean during the course of the Hapsburg-Valois wars. Their raids, carried out both by French Protestants and by the Catholic government, culminated in an attack on Havana in 1555. Further, they planned to seize the silver bullion stored at Nombre de Dios in Panama before marching across the Isthmus to capture the Spanish treasure fleet. The French abandoned this scheme only because the wars between France and Spain ended in 1559 when both sides ran out of money. The peace talks provided the first forum for a discussion about the rights of European governments in American territory, but the diplomats could not agree on any official positions. Thus, while the resulting Treaty of Cateau-Cambresis said nothing about America, European monarchs recognized an informal understanding that in areas west of the prime meridian and south of the Tropic of Cancer, "might made right," and ships sailed at their own risk. They agreed that despite what happened within Europe, there would be, in a famous phrase, "no peace beyond the line."

The end of the Hapsburg-Valois wars, however, did not end France's hostility to Spain. While a series of religious civil wars between Protestants and Catholics prevented France from following any consistent imperial policy after 1562, French Protestants showed that colonies played a potentially vital role in European wars and that they also served as safe havens for the "true faith" in dangerous times. At the same time, these religious wars intensified attacks by French pirates. Both Catholics and Protestants strengthened their navies in attempts to destroy the enemy's trade and to ruin its ability to receive aid. In the late sixteenth century, for example, French Catholics attacked ships bound for the Protestant port of La Rochelle, while Protestants tried to blockade Catholic ports. French Protestants also continued to follow an overall strategy to weaken Catholic Spain by capturing its treasure fleets and by establishing bases of operation to offset Spanish domination of America.

During the first half of the 1560s, enterprising Frenchmen attempted to execute their plans with settlements along the Atlantic coast of Florida. In 1562 Jacques Ribault attempted to organize a Protestant foothold in Florida. By establishing a colony at Port Royal (now Battery Creek, South Carolina), he hoped to control the route by which the Spanish treasure ships left the Gulf of Mexico. Gaspard de Coligny, an influential Protestant and government minister, backed the plan because he thought the colony might be useful in the global struggle against Spain and Catholicism, and as an outlet for the dangerous ambitions and energy of unemployed French soldiers. The French eventually abandoned the settlement, however, and Ribault, who had been seeking reinforcements in France, had to flee to England for safety. While there he devised a plan for a joint Anglo-French attack on Spanish Florida, but the Spaniards learned about the plot and managed to thwart it. The French resurrected the project in 1564, however, when René de Laudonnière led three hundred soldiers and colonists to establish Fort Caroline, near modern Jacksonville, Florida. Despite disagreements among the colonists over treatment of Native Americans, and the general reluctance of the French colonists to perform any agricultural work, provisions supplied by an English expedition and the reappearance of Ribault—with reinforcements—promised to save the day. The prospect of a successful French colony close to Spanish trade routes proved intolerable to Spain. In 1565, a Spanish military force destroyed the French colony and massacred the colonists. In revenge, another French Protestant force surprised and overthrew three Spanish forts in Florida, much to the embarrassment of France's Catholic rulers.

After this episode, the French made no more attempts to penetrate the heartland of the Spanish empire with permanent colonies. Yet, their attempts to weaken the Spanish presence in America continued. Over the next half century, French pirates attacked Spanish interests in the Atlantic and the Gulf of Mexico, threatening Panama in 1571 and Peru in 1595. The French also combined war with trade. In the 1560s they operated on the Venezuelan coast, in Panama, and in the Caribbean islands, illegally supplying the needs of settlers in the more remote Spanish settlements. Spain complained of this "continual trade" in 1570, as French traders offered African slaves and French textiles in exchange for tobacco and sugar. By the end of the century, the French constituted the major foreign presence in the Antilles.

The French also tried to strike a blow against Spanish and Portuguese power in South America. In the 1530s, King Francis I, hoping for Portuguese support against Spain, had repeatedly prohibited his subjects from trespassing in Portuguese West Africa. By the middle of the sixteenth century, however, French sailors and entrepreneurs conducted a vigorous trade between West Africa, the Caribbean, and Brazil, which the French had known about since at least 1504. At midcentury, they established outposts for loading Brazilwood and cotton in areas not under Portuguese control. French sailors became so familiar with the route to Brazil that others who wished to trade there, such as the English, frequently employed them as navigators.

In 1555 the French boldly attempted to colonize an island in the bay of Rio de Janeiro, in the very heart of Portuguese territory. Under the bold leadership of an experienced soldier, Nicolas Durand, Chevalier de Villegaignon, this colony included both Catholics and Protestants, something no other European government had allowed to happen. Predictably, the colony failed primarily because Protestants and Catholics fought bitterly with each other in this hostile environment. Villegaignon, unable to heal the religious divisions, abandoned the colony. In 1560, a Portuguese military force captured the settlement, but the survivors escaped to the mainland where, with help from Native Americans, they lived for several more years.

After this fiasco, the French attempted to settle in northeastern Brazil and on the coasts of Maranhão and Paría, but with little success. With the exception of Cayenne (in 1604), the Portuguese destroyed these colonies as well. French traders persisted where French colonists did not, however, and in the late sixteenth century other Europeans reported meeting, or hearing of, French ships in Brazil. One of these encounters involved seven French ships that had gone to trade with the "wild people" and had been destroyed by the Portuguese.

Unlike France, England based its colonial policies, at least at first, on a good relationship with Spain and the Hapsburgs. To strengthen the alliance between Spain and England, King Henry VII arranged a marriage between his eldest son, Arthur, and Catherine of Aragon, a daughter of Ferdinand and Isabella. When Arthur died prematurely, the English king secured the pope's approval to marry his second son, the future Henry VIII, to the same woman. Later, Henry VIII's eldest daughter, Mary Tudor, married King Philip II of Spain.

In the early sixteenth century, the city of Bristol dominated English maritime activity. Its sailors, searching for new fishing grounds, may have reached Newfoundland as early as the 1480s. Perhaps inspired by reports of these voyages, the Venetian John Cabot (Giovanni Caboto) appeared in England around 1495; and like Columbus, he proposed to find a westward route to Asia. Aided by modest financial support, he eventually sailed from Bristol and made a landfall (in 1497) either in Labrador, Newfoundland, or Maine. Despite the fact that Cabot never returned from his second expedition, many other explorers set sail for North America in the early sixteenth century. One of these later voyagers, John Cabot's son, Sebastian, also tried—but failed—to reach Asia by finding a passage through what was coming to be recognized as a new continent.

Although the Cabots failed to reach Asia by going west, English interest in North America persisted and grew rapidly. In 1521 King Henry VIII attempted to involve skeptical London merchants in one of Sebastian Cabot's expeditions. Six years later, the king commissioned another expedition charged with finding a passage to Asia somewhere between Newfoundland and Labrador. Although the expedition found no such strait, it explored the American coast as far south as the Caribbean. Yet, apart from a disastrous expedition to Labrador and Newfoundland in 1536, these early efforts ceased because the coastline of northern America appeared inhospitable and the natives displayed no gold, silver, or anything else to make the effort worthwhile. Moreover, the English government simply could not challenge Spanish power in the Caribbean, especially if it wanted to maintain good relations with the Hapsburgs. Accordingly, the English government ignored a proposal for a voyage to the Spice Islands in 1530 and for an expedition to China in 1540.

During the middle decades of the sixteenth century, England endured a political and religious crisis which made the country more aggressive and disrupted the traditional alliance with Spain. After Henry VIII created the Church of England in 1534, his children, King Edward VI (1547–53) and Queen Mary (1553–58), turned the country first Protestant and then Catholic. Protestants fled to the safety of the European continent, especially to Calvin's Geneva, during Mary's reign, but they returned home to enjoy the toleration provided by her sister Elizabeth who became the new queen (1558–1603). A hard core of these Protestants, the Puritans, became relentless enemies of Catholicism—and willing allies of any enemy of Catholic Spain. With the liberal Protestant favoritism of Queen Elizabeth, the good relations that England had shared with the Hapsburgs now came to an end, and hostility between the two families became a key element in English foreign policy. At the same time, the market for English textiles in the Hapsburg-controlled Netherlands collapsed; and after several years of friction with the Hapsburgs there, the English merchant community withdrew from the region in 1564. Clearly, English merchants needed new markets, and this too brought England into conflict with its former ally.

To compensate for their lost Netherlands market, and to attack Catholic Spain, English sailors began to look to the Atlantic trade for profits. In 1562, John Hawkins, commanding a fleet of both private and government ships, and with powerful London, naval, and government support, attempted to break into the African slave trade to the Americas. He obtained the slaves he needed by intervening in an African tribal war and sold them to Spanish colonists in the Caribbean. After several other illegal commercial ventures, however, the Spanish treasure fleet trapped Hawkins's ships in San Juan de Ulúa (near Vera Cruz, Mexico). Although he escaped, he had already found the Caribbean market to be one of the least prosperous in the Americas and the least able to afford his cargoes. Moreover, Hawkins had to compete with the French and Portuguese traders, who were considerably aided by countrymen already settled in the area.

To many contemporary observers, Hawkins's activity seemed to illustrate typical English habits. Indeed, Europeans regarded England as little more than a nest of seafaring thieves. England turned these talents against Spain, however, in a war which reached its climax in Elizabeth's reign. As early as 1533, English voyagers planned to capture a Spanish treasure fleet; by the 1540s, English attacks on Spanish shipping in the English channel resembled open warfare. Soon after Elizabeth became queen, her government abandoned these random attacks in favor of a deliberate policy which would enrich England and cripple Spain. Following France's example, the English attacked Spanish shipping in the Atlantic and the Caribbean. This policy particularly appealed to English ship owners who willingly transferred their acts of piracy from nearby waters to the western Atlantic Ocean and Caribbean Sea.

Under Elizabethan protection, Francis Drake became the key figure in the new English strategy. Like many of his countrymen, he took his Protestant religion seriously. He carried a copy of John Foxe's *Book of Martyrs* (a record of the suffering and execution of Protestants in England during Mary's reign) with him and read extracts from it to his Spanish prisoners. In the early 1570s, he raided Spanish settlements in the Caribbean, establishing a base on an isolated stretch of the coast of Panama. Although he twice failed to capture the Spanish treasure fleets, even with French help, he succeeded in capturing a Spanish mule-train carrying silver bullion near Nombre de Dios in 1573. Three years after this first, successful, English military attack on the mainland of Spanish America, another Englishman, John Oxenham, crossed the Isthmus of Panama and reached the Isle of Pearls. From this post until his capture soon after arriving, he controlled the approaches to Panama in hopes of waylaying a Peruvian silver shipment.

At first Spain did not allow such events to damage seriously its relations with England. Philip II had more pressing problems, and the legal trade between the countries constituted an important component for both economies. Nevertheless, England's zealous Protestants and naval administrators advocated even stronger action against Spain. They wanted to capture the islands of Cuba and Hispaniola, establish a colony near the southern tip of South America from which Spanish settlements in Peru could be attacked, and to do more to disrupt the flow of precious metals from America to Spain. In 1577 Drake commanded a fleet of ships financed by private and public resources officially bound for Egypt. Undoubtedly, he sailed with instructions to examine both sides of the southern tip of South America, contact natives known to be enemies of the Spaniards there, and evaluate the prospects for an attack on Peru. Investors anticipated that this exploration would be paid for by the capture of Spanish ships. As it turned out, Drake sailed around the world before he was finished with the mission, returning home in 1580 as the first commander to complete a circumnavigation of the earth (Magellan had been killed by natives in the Philippines on his voyage in the 1520s). Along the way, Drake attacked Spanish settlements on the Pacific coast of South America and captured a Spanish treasure ship. Drake had shown the English that the riches of the Pacific region were now open to them and that the claims of Portugal (conquered by Spain in 1580) in Asia could be safely ignored. Not surprisingly, English relations with Spain deteriorated badly after 1580.

Now that the lucrative trade between the two countries seemed to be coming to an end, England began a series of official raids against Spanish shipping. Until Elizabeth's death in 1603, the English launched over seventy expeditions to plunder Spanish settlements in the Atlantic and the Caribbean. Philip responded to English attacks in 1585 by seizing English ships in Spanish ports, and in the same year, Drake—with twenty-two ships and over two thousand men, the strongest force yet to attack the Spanish empire—sacked Santiago, Chile; took Santo Domingo; pillaged Cartagena, Colombia; and attacked Florida. More audaciously, before he did all this, he attacked the coast of Spain, itself. Drake not only had struck a blow at Spanish commerce, he had done much damage to Spain's morale and international prestige. In 1587 Drake launched yet another attack on Spain, this time sailing into the Spanish port of Cadiz to sink thirty-seven new war ships and thereby disrupt preparations for a retaliatory attack on England.

Vexed by these insults and other defeats, and by England's continuing association with Spain's rebellious subjects in the Netherlands, Spain dispatched a mighty armada of ships to crush

England in 1588. This represented the most ambitious and difficult naval operation ever undertaken by a European country. Its success depended on the cooperation of the Dutch, the unpredictable weather in the English Channel, and ability of two military commanders—the prince of Parma on land and the duke of Medina-Sidonia at sea—to work together harmoniously. Everything favored the English: they had more ships (105 to 71), they enjoyed an immense superiority in firepower, and even had the weather behind them. Spain lost at least 50 of its ships, suffered a crushing blow to its prestige, and for all of its effort, accomplished nothing.

Although the English had now established themselves as Europe's finest sailors, they had not really ruined Spain. Moreover, they failed to take full advantage of their victory, and their subsequent strategy lacked an overall direction: John Hawkins wanted to establish a naval blockade to cut off Spain's supply of American silver; Queen Elizabeth favored an expedition to Spain to destroy what remained of the Armada; and Francis Drake believed that Portugal could be persuaded to rebel against Spanish rule. This divided objective produced the inevitable— an expedition in 1589 under a divided command and with no specific goal. Drake led a large force (150 ships and about twenty thousand men) against the Spanish city of Coruña, but with little effect. Indeed, after this fiasco, Drake received no significant command for the next six years. Hawkins did no better. His blockade interrupted the flow of American silver to Spain only temporarily, while the Spaniards defeated an English fleet in 1591. After this, Elizabeth became reluctant to risk her own ships. English successes against Spain became rare at the end of the century, with an attack on the Spanish city of Cadiz in 1596 standing as the most notable victory.

Against this background, Drake and Hawkins launched their last expedition against Spain in 1595. Their fleet comprised both private and royal ships, but lacked a clear objective. Once again, Elizabeth wanted to hinder Spanish preparations for a second Armada, while Drake and Hawkins preferred to raid Panama for their own profit. Drake and Hawkins got their way, but this time the Spaniards were ready for them. They repulsed the English attack, and killed both English commanders. After this, English pirates continued harassing Spanish ships and carrying on an illegal trade with Spanish colonists in the Caribbean. At the same time, Spanish defenses improved, so the geographical range of English pirates' activities had to be extended. When the English war against Spain officially ended in 1604, many Englishmen continued their activities on their own. Although they never captured a treasure fleet, in the eighteen years of war (1586–1604) between the two countries, the English captured over one thousand Spanish and Portuguese ships. In the Caribbean, the English had penetrated an area vital to the interests of the Hapsburgs. Their raids, together with those of the French and the Dutch, forced the Spanish government to take expensive defensive measures.

By the end of the sixteenth century, England clearly had defeated Spain at sea. In the Caribbean they had penetrated to the heart of the Hapsburg overseas empire. The Spanish king Philip II had failed to conquer England or return it to the Catholic faith, while the English continued to attack the Spanish coast and settlements in America. Many reasons account for England's success in the war against Spain: An important one is that Spain had to defend its far-flung empire, not only against the English and the French, but also from the Dutch.

By the early seventeenth century, Holland benefitted more than any other nation from Spain's decline. In little more than half a century, the Dutch Republic not only had won its independence from Spain, but in the process it had risen from relative insignificance to become a major European power. During the Middle Ages, the Netherlands constituted part of the lands ruled by the dukes of Burgundy. Through dynastic intermarriage, the Hapsburgs inherited these lands, but inhabitants of the Netherlands converted to Protestantism in the early 1500s and resented Spanish attempts to rule them more efficiently. General resistance to Spanish rule broke into open rebellion during the last half of the sixteenth century. After prolonged fighting, the Spanish government tacitly recognized Dutch independence in the truce of 1609, but it did not grant formal independence until 1648.

During their war for independence, at least up until the truce of 1609, the Dutch contemplated attacking Spanish treasure fleets, cooperated with their English allies against the Spanish

Armada, and even mounted some naval campaigns in Spanish waters. These official campaigns against Spain, however, turned out to be much less effective than the efforts of Dutch privateers (pirates). Pirates from the Netherlands had sailed the Atlantic for some time; and as early as the 1540s, English sailors complained about Dutch piracy. By the middle of Queen Elizabeth's reign, the boldness of the Dutch brigands caused her to send a squadron of ships to drive them from the English channel. The Dutch remained steadfast, however, and their ships continued attacking all others, including English vessels, which they suspected of trading with Spain or its allies. Indeed, the Dutch took advantage of the 1609 truce to increase their attacks on Spanish settlements in the Atlantic and the Caribbean.

After the expiration of the twelve years' truce in 1621, the conflict between the Netherlands, Spain, and Portugal increasingly focused in the region of the Americas. In fact, the Spanish government decided to resume its war with the Netherlands in 1621 not only because it wanted to end a rebellion that had already lasted for over half a century, it also wanted to protect its overseas interests from Dutch assaults. Spanish officials argued that the renewal of war in Europe would reduce Dutch opportunities to attack Spanish and Portuguese colonies in America. In this case, they reasoned incorrectly.

In 1624 the Dutch successfully attacked and occupied the Portuguese settlement of Bahia in Brazil. The Spaniards recognized the need to counterattack as quickly as possible for several very good reasons. The development of Portugal's Atlantic empire, based on the rapid expansion of the Brazilian sugar-growing industry, helped to compensate for the loss of its Asian trade to the Dutch. From the time Spain conquered Portugal in 1580, it had a vital interest in keeping its colonial empire intact. Unfortunately, the Portuguese had been defeated in the East despite the military strength of Spain. If the Portuguese were now to suffer defeat in Brazil as well, the union of Spain and Portugal might be further weakened. Therefore, in 1625 the Spanish government sent a combined Spanish and Portuguese military force to recapture Bahia, which it did, easily.

Frustrated in Brazil, the Dutch reacted in two ways. First, they returned to the Caribbean where their powerful fleets again launched fullscale naval operations against Spain's treasure ships. In 1628, the Dutch commander Piet Heyn—a former Spanish galley slave—captured the Spanish treasure fleet. The Dutch also seized several islands to use as bases of operations against Spain. The most important of these, Tortuga, Bonaire, Aruba, and Curaçao, were of great economic significance. The Dutch sold cloth from Tortuga throughout the Gulf of Mexico, raised maize on Bonaire and horses on Aruba, and sold African slaves to Spanish and other colonists from Curaçao. Second, still coveting the wealth of Brazil (sugar, dyewood, and cotton), they began illegal trading in the area. They established partnerships with Portuguese merchants, usually new converts to Christianity from Judaism, or worked together with Portuguese Jewish refugees in Holland who maintained their contacts with Portuguese Jews. Through these contacts, Dutch ships carried about two-thirds of the trade between Brazil and Europe in the 1620s.

The Spanish treasure captured by Heyn helped finance new Dutch attacks on the Spaniards and Portuguese. By 1640, captured Spanish gold had not only helped the Dutch achieve a prominent position among European nations, but it had also financed the Dutch contribution to the decline of the Spanish empire in Europe and America. In 1630, for example, the Dutch attacked the Portuguese colony at Pernambuco, in Brazil. This time, Spain lacked the necessary resources to get the Dutch out before they became established there. Within fifteen years the Dutch controlled about half of the colony, including the best sugar-growing regions. In addition, Dutch occupation of northeastern Brazil in the 1630s had serious consequences for Spanish foreign policy in Europe. On the one hand, the Spanish government eagerly wanted to conclude peace with the Netherlands because it faced the prospect of a war with France; on the other hand, Spain could not simply abandon Brazil to the Dutch because that would alienate Spain's Portuguese allies.

To make matters even more serious for Spain, its relationship with Portugal had deteriorated in the 1630s. Portuguese merchants had successfully entered into the economies of both Spain and its colonies in America, producing a hostility towards Portugal in both places. Moreover, the defense of Portugal's interests in Brazil proved to be a financial and military burden for Spain.

For their part, the Portuguese found out that they were not welcome in Spanish America at the same time that they faced the loss of their possessions in Brazil. As a result, many Portuguese came to believe that they would be well-served by independence from Spain. An independent Portuguese empire, based on settlements in Africa and Brazil, might well substitute for the declining Spanish empire to which they were bound.

Events in Europe and America combined effectively in 1639–40 to destroy Spain's pretensions as a world power. The financial strain imposed by Spain's war with France totally paralyzed Seville's trade with America. At the same time, the Spanish navy suffered defeats in the North Atlantic and off the coast of Brazil. Clearly, Spain had lost control of the seas. Not a single treasure fleet reached Seville in 1640, compounding the economic crisis. In the spring of 1640, the Spanish province of Catalonia revolted against the government; in the summer, Spanish armies met defeat in the Netherlands; and in the winter, Portugal proclaimed its independence. As a consequence, the deterioration of Spanish power in Europe left its Caribbean colonies wide open for new assaults by the French, English, and the Dutch. After a century and a half, the Spanish economic monopoly over America, awarded by papal decrees and the Treaty of Tordesillas in the mid 1490s, finally came to an end. During the same period, Spain's philosophic and moral justification for New World dominance came under attack.

Various European states fought for their share of the riches of America with words as well as weapons. These propaganda battles are important because they allow us to understand how the existence of America penetrated the European mentality in the Renaissance. To the Spaniards, for example, the exploration and conquest of America demonstrated that they were chosen by God to bring Christianity and civilization to Native Americans. By the end of the sixteenth century, however, it became clear that other Europeans also cherished the notion that they had an important civilizing mission to accomplish in America. By encouraging the European desire for treasure, trade, and colonies, and by making the acquisition of its wealth part of a divinely inspired mission, America stimulated the nationalistic beliefs of Renaissance Europeans. At the same time, events in America themselves provided new images and events on which national and religious hatreds could thrive. The offenses committed by one European power against another soon entered the collective imaginations of both sides—as either victories to be savored or defeats to be avenged.

At the start of the Age of Exploration, Pope Alexander VI, Ferdinand and Isabella, Christopher Columbus, and a majority of the other explorers proclaimed officially that they were chiefly motivated by the noble purpose of bringing Christianity to Native Americans. To some observers, however, the behavior of many Spaniards towards the natives proved most unsatisfactory, and they complained bitterly to Ferdinand and Isabella. The most violent and persistent of these critics, the Dominican Bartolomé de Las Casas (the "Protector of the Indians"), did more than anyone in history to create and fix in the European consciousness the so-called Black Legend of Spanish cruelty.

Las Casas condemned the Spanish conquest of America and declared that Spain had no right to exploit Native Americans in any way. While he supported attempts to convert the natives to Christianity, he believed that the use of force was wrong in this case. Conversion should be based on love, but the Spaniards in America were tyrants and destroyers. In particular, Las Casas objected strongly to Spaniards who abused native laborers granted to them in the *encomienda* system. The behavior of his countrymen, he believed, constituted a scandal in the eyes of God, and he wanted the Spanish government to promulgate laws that would stop it. Although he succeeded in having laws passed which were designed to protect Native Americans, they often proved impractical; in some cases they were simply ignored. Nevertheless, the knowledge that the Spanish government was concerned about treating the natives justly served to control the worst excesses of individual Spaniards.

Las Casas's anger over the treatment of the natives began with his own observations of the cruelties perpetrated by Spanish settlers in Hispaniola and Cuba. His father, Pedro de Las Casas, had gone to Hispaniola on Columbus's second voyage, and Bartolomé himself arrived with the newly appointed governor, Nicolas de Ovando, in 1502. Ovando had received careful instructions about the treatment of natives from Queen Isabella.

She had told him that her main goal in governing these new territories was to convert Native Americans to Christianity. She also gave Ovando the authority to force the natives to live together with the Spaniards and to work for them on their farms and in their mines. Nevertheless, Isabella insisted that Native Americans were free people, not slaves.

After Isabella's death in 1504, her husband Ferdinand became ruler of the Spanish possessions in the Americas. One of Europe's most cynical rulers, he cared less about converting his new subjects to Christianity than about exploiting their labor and taking their gold. Indeed, when natives started dying in large numbers, he authorized slaving expeditions against "cannibals" to increase the work force in the mines, and he authorized the removal of whole tribes from the Bahamas to Hispaniola for that purpose. Witnessing what was happening, Las Casas sailed home to Spain in 1515 to urge the king to do something to save Native Americans from destruction. From this point on, Las Casas became the defender of Native Americans' rights.

A Dominican friar named Antonio Montesinos accompanied Las Casas on this voyage. Four years earlier, Montesinos had preached a sermon in Santo Domingo denouncing Spanish treatment of Native Americans. This was the first important attack by the Dominicans, although others had already complained of similar conditions. In the following year, 1512, Montesinos had returned to Spain to appeal directly to Ferdinand. Montesinos apparently convinced Ferdinand of the horrors suffered by Native Americans because the king convened a council of scholars and theologians to devise a law code to handle the situation. Proclaimed in the Spanish city of Burgos in 1512, these so-called Laws of Burgos attempted to protect Native Americans and remained in force for the next thirty years. Although these laws limited the number of natives a Spaniard could hold as slaves to 150, they also legalized forced labor.

Now, in 1515, Las Casas and Montesinos again traveled to Spain to protest that the Laws of Burgos had not stopped the bad treatment of Native Americans. Having seen this with their own eyes, they intended to try to correct government policy and see that evildoers were punished. Ferdinand met with Las

Casas once, in November of 1515, and agreed to see him again after Christmas. They never met again—Ferdinand died in January, 1516. Now Las Casas appealed to the two government officials who effectively ruled Spain's American possessions: Juan de Fonseca, Bishop of Burgos and head of the Casa de Contratacíon, and Lope de Conchillos, secretary of the Council of Castile. Neither of these men were concerned about what Las Casas had to say.

Las Casas turned to Cardinal Francisco de Ximenes and Adrian of Utrecht, who served as representatives of the new Spanish king, Charles I (later Holy Roman Emperor Charles V), who was still living in Flanders. His written report on the condition of the natives so shocked them that they called a council to consider what should be done. Las Casas wanted Native Americans to be free from forced labor. Cardinal Ximenes agreed. He gave Las Casas the title "Protector of the Indians," and authorized him to select three clergymen to go to the Indies to institute reforms. They devised an elaborate plan to resettle the natives in their own villages (but under Spanish supervision). Nevertheless, they accomplished little; their plans did not work out in practice.

Back in Spain, Las Casas finally persuaded King Charles to establish a free commonwealth for Native Americans. Las Casas himself would govern it. He received a grant of territory on the coast of Venezuela and the right to recruit Spanish settlers— to be known as the "Knights of the Golden Spur." Las Casas even designed a uniform for them to wear: a white robe with a red cross on the front (Las Casas later admitted that he was the only one who ever wore it). In theory, the Spaniards would live among the natives and teach them to work hard and be conscientious Christians through their good examples. Set up in 1520, Las Casas's bold enterprise failed miserably. By 1521, the natives in his settlement had revolted and killed two friars. In retaliation, a Spanish expedition enslaved Native Americans whom it could capture there. In the meantime the Knights of the Golden Spur themselves joined other raiding expeditions.

Discouraged by the failure of his noble effort, Las Casas retired to a Dominican monastery in 1522 and then dropped out of sight for almost a decade. In 1531, he drew up a statement to the

Council of the Indies describing the brutal Spanish treatment of the natives. On Hispaniola alone, he asserted, more than a million natives had been slaughtered by Spaniards, and he described in detail how it had been done. Ten years later, in 1541, Las Casas began the most extensive propaganda campaign of his career. His vivid descriptions of the cruelties inflicted upon Native Americans (technically subjects of the Spanish government) paved the way for the famous "New Laws," which Charles approved in 1542.

The New Laws ordered a reform in the administration of Spanish territories in America and laid down new regulations for the treatment of Native Americans. Henceforth, no natives could be enslaved, even those captured in war, and government officials became the direct supervisors of all Native Americans. The New Laws exempted from all service those natives who survived in Hispaniola, Puerto Rico, and Cuba, where the death rates had been highest, so that they might recuperate and multiply. The Laws also spelled out in detail the proper treatment of Native Americans. Although the New Laws were not as drastic as Las Casas might have wished, they did eliminate *encomiendas* (through which the Spanish government gave native laborers to colonists). His ideas also found support in Rome, where the papal bull *Sublimis Deus* (1537) condemned as heretical the opinion that Native Americans were irrational and therefore incapable of receiving the faith.

Less than three weeks after the appearance of the New Laws, Las Casas completed his most famous book, *The Brief Account of the Destruction of the Indies*. It had an enormous influence in persuading Europeans, especially Spain's enemies, that Spanish atrocities towards the natives were as bad as anyone could have imagined. With the intensification of religious divisions in late sixteenth century Europe, Las Casas's work became a potent propaganda tool. In 1578, it was translated into Dutch, and in 1579, Jacques de Miggrode translated it into French (this version was translated into English in 1583). The preface of the English edition declared that the book was designed to serve as a precedent and warning to the seventeen provinces of the Netherlands. Indeed, the English translator retained the loaded phrases of Miggrode's subtitle: *Spanish cruelties and tyrannies, perpetrated in the West Indies, commonly called the new found world.*

The anonymous English translator clearly wanted to make the most of the attack on the Spaniards, whom he delightedly condemned by the writings of one of their own priests. Region by region, Las Casas detailed the cruelties and destruction brought by his countrymen. This grim story reached a climax in Las Casas's description of the slaughter of the inhabitants of Peru. He included direct quotations from a priest who claimed to have been an eyewitness to the cruelties: thousands burned, others cut down by swords, and many mutilated by having their hands, ears, and noses cut off. He declared that women and children were killed merely out of a desire to annoy their husbands and fathers; babies were snatched from their mothers' breasts and flung to their deaths, some to bloodthirsty dogs.

The Italian explorer and writer Girolamo Benzoni also provided similar descriptions of Spanish atrocities towards Native Americans in his *History of the New World* (1565). A Latin translation of Benzoni's book appeared in Geneva—the center of the Calvinist movement—in 1578, while a French translation followed in 1579. At the same time a graphic and sensational account of a 1563 massacre of French Calvinists by Spanish Catholics in Florida also appeared in Geneva. By the 1580s, therefore, the most lurid accounts of Spanish conduct in America circulated among the European reading public. They needed only the horrific illustrations included in the German edition of Las Casas's *Brief Account*, published by the Protestant Theodore De Bry at the end of the century, to stamp an unforgettable image of Spanish atrocities on the European consciousness.

The Protestants, especially the English and the Dutch, seized on Las Casas and Benzoni's works with delight. In his *Apology*, William of Orange, the leader of the Dutch revolt against Spain in 1581, cited the destruction of some twenty million natives by the Spaniards as evidence of the "natural" predisposition of Spaniards to commit acts of great cruelty. Now Protestants could claim that they were doing God's work in punishing such sinful tyrants. Against propaganda warfare on this grand scale, Spanish historians could offer only feeble arguments. For the first time in European history, the enemies of an imperial power systematically used its colonial record against it.

The acquisition of overseas territories and the creation of empires not only influenced the foreign policies of European states, but they also contributed to changes in the relationship between rulers and their subjects at home. European governments became more powerful during the Age of Exploration. Indeed, only strong governments could marshal the resources, strength, and unity of purpose to successfully exploit overseas possessions—often at the expense of other, competing, centralized European states.

Spain provides the best illustration of how the exploration and conquest of America increased the power of European governments, especially in the sphere of church-state relations. In the 1490s, Pope Alexander VI had charged Ferdinand and Isabella with the task of bringing Christianity to Native Americans. Although this might appear to offer the Church a God-given opportunity to increase its authority, the actual result turned out to be quite the opposite. By accepting the sacred obligation to convert the natives, Ferdinand and Isabella, and their successors, obtained important concessions from the pope to help them in their holy work.

No Christian missionary could bring the message of God to the natives without the help, and sometimes the military support, of the government. This could be dangerous work. As one of these missionaries, José de Acosta, put it, for missionaries to trust themselves to the mercy of Native Americans was like trying to make friends with wild boars or crocodiles (see page 55). The Spanish government took advantage of the fearful situation of missionaries to dictate how missionary activity should proceed. It gained authority over almost all religious matters in its American possessions. Indeed, the neglect of American affairs in the discussions at the Council of Trent, in the middle of the sixteenth century, reflects the pope's diminishing influence over missionary work in America.

At that time, the Spanish historian Francisco López de Gómara referred to his king as the "absolute lord of the Indies." Indeed, there can be little doubt that the Spanish conquest of America increased the power of the Spanish government in domestic affairs as well. Although it is difficult to prove, historians suspect that the growth of Spanish governmental power at home closely followed its increasing authority overseas. The government certainly benefitted from its overseas activity. It enjoyed the exclusive right to authorize all expeditions of exploration and conquest in the Americas and to fill all of the administrative, judicial, and ecclesiastical offices there as it saw fit. By the 1550s, for example, the Spanish government had appointed twenty-two bishops and archbishops in America. Of even greater importance, it acquired vast new sources of income, based on its claim to the soil and subsoil of the newly conquered lands. In order to effectively exploit these resources, the government created an elaborate bureaucracy which managed to exercise a reasonable degree of authority despite its deficiencies and the inefficient systems of communication and transportation at the time.

In its struggle to assert its authority at home, the Spanish government benefitted from its overseas activity. It gained prestige from being associated with the divine mission for the conversion of the natives, immense new powers of patronage, and, of course, vast new economic resources as well. At the same time, historians believe that the problems associated with domestic conflict may have been reduced by the government's possession of overseas, and distant, territories which could provide an outlet for the energies of "unruly" elements in the population. The point seemed clear to foreigners who compared the unrest in their own countries to the peace and tranquility that they perceived in Spain. In 1582, for example, the French Protestant historian Henri Lancelot Voisin, sieur de la Popelinière, declared that if Spain had not sent all of its "rogues" to America after the war against the Moslems in Granada, they would have caused great unrest in the country. Moreover, he urged the French government to establish overseas colonies for the same reason—to get rid of people who were useful during wars but who disturb the peace of the realm in peacetime. Another Frenchman, Admiral Gaspard de Coligny, repeated the belief that at least some of France's domestic troubles might be worked out if the people causing the problems could be sent away to distant colonies.

Richard Hakluyt, the great sixteenth-century English advocate of colonization and empire, echoed these sentiments when he declared that a great colonial enterprise would help England because it would remove the unmanageable surplus population. Indeed, the emigration of the undesirable part of the population from Europe to America seemed to strengthen the prospects for strong centralized government at home. The countries with overseas possessions seemed to enjoy the most peaceful domestic conditions.

POLITICAL THOUGHT

When European governments established overseas empires, they encountered difficult problems concerning colonial adminis-tration and political theory. In the sixteenth century, Spain led the rest of Europe not only in the development of colonial administration but also in the field of political thought. Spanish lawyers defined the notion of governmental power in various ways during the Renaissance, and in so doing they provoked a good deal of discussion about that topic. When Spain extended its power to America, the subject of the proper role of govern-ment authority became even more complex.

The Spanish government based its right to rule in America on the papal bulls of 1493, which granted to Spain those "islands and mainlands" not already held by Christian rulers. None of the territories subsequently colonized by the Spaniards in America had Christian rulers, of course, but native peoples inhabited all these areas. Although some of the inhabitants were very primitive by European standards, they all seemed to rec-ognize and obey some form of political leadership. Different European intellectuals came to different conclusions over the question of the legitimacy of Native American political authority, however, and they also disagreed over the pope's right to award political power in America to any European government. Some Europeans, especially Protestants, realized they could not re-alistically expect Native Americans to recognize the authority of the pope. Moral, intellectual, and legal questions about the exercise of power in America by Europeans had to be settled in other ways.

The fact that few Europeans in 1493 entertained any serious doubts about the pope's spiritual authority made the question of European power in America more difficult to solve. The papal bulls of 1493 clearly instructed the Spanish government to try to convert Native Americans to Christianity. Who could deny the right of the pope to charge the Spanish government with doing that? And who could deny the duty of the Spanish government to carry out the pope's wishes? Nevertheless, difficult questions remained about the extent to which Spanish authorities should use political or military power to achieve this spiritual objective. Did the duty of conversion justify the military conquest of Native Americans, the overthrow of their leaders, or the declaration of Spanish supremacy over the them? These central issues engaged the efforts of the best legal scholars in the sixteenth century.

Perhaps the most important single individual in the development of the concept of international law is the Spaniard Francisco de Vitoria. After studying in Paris for nearly eighteen years, he returned to Spain where he taught theology at the University of Salamanca. Unlike most distinguished university professors, Vitoria published virtually nothing during his long and distinguished academic career, so we know about his ideas only from summaries of his lectures. Nevertheless, Vitoria won an excellent reputation as a teacher, and by the time of his death in 1546 nearly thirty of his students held professorships in Spanish universities.

Vitoria's reputation comes from a series of public lectures at Salamanca in the 1530s, in which he defended Native Americans against their Spanish conquerors. At the time, the lectures caused a sensation. His most famous lecture, entitled *The Recently Discovered Indies*, considered two crucial questions about native society: did Native Americans have a genuine political society with valid rulers? and did they possess private property and real estate before the arrival of the Spaniards? To both of these questions Vitoria answered yes. He argued that there can be no doubt that Native Americans possessed real authority both in public and private affairs, and, further, that the Spaniards could not legitimately overthrow native rulers or take away the property of Native Americans.

Vitoria also provided a basis for undermining the Spanish justification of their conquest of Native Americans. He clearly dismissed the argument that the pope had granted to Spaniards the right to hold power in America. Even if Native Americans refused to recognize the authority of the pope in this matter, he thought, this fact did not constitute a valid reason for the Spaniards to make war on them or seize their property. According to Vitoria, the pope simply did not have the right to give such power over the natives to the Spaniards in the first place. He also denied the suggestion that the Spaniards could legitimately make war on the natives in order to force them to convert to Christianity. In this case, Vitoria claimed that all human beings possessed an equal ability to establish and maintain their own political societies, whether they were Christian or not. Indeed, he concluded that even if Native Americans rejected the teachings of Christian missionaries, the Spaniards still could not wage a lawful war against them or take their property.

Although Vitoria rejected both papal and Spanish claims to exercise power over Native Americans, he nevertheless recognized some ambiguities in the relationship between Europeans and Native Americans. In some circumstances, Spaniards could interfere in Native Americans' affairs. For example, he found such customs as cannibalism and human sacrifice simply unacceptable, and insisted that Spaniards had the right to use their power to prevent the natives from practicing them. Despite their rationality, Native Americans could not govern themselves adequately, Vitoria believed, because they had no proper legal systems or magistrates to enforce laws. Therefore, Spaniards could act as administrators for Native Americans but only for the benefit of the Native Americans. Under certain circumstances, Spaniards could also ally militarily with one tribe of natives and wage war legitimately against another tribe. Finally, Vitoria asserted that Spaniards and Native Americans could trade with each other, and that Spaniards could travel freely in America as long as they did so peacefully.

During the middle decades of the sixteenth century, political theorists bombarded the Spanish government with advice on colonial policy, and the governing of American possessions became the subject of a bitter propaganda war. The participants in this contest fell into two camps: those who wanted to protect the natives' freedom and those who thought that Europeans should have power over them. The most famous advocates of these positions were, respectively, Bartolomé de Las Casas and Juan Ginés de Sepúlveda.

Las Casas's thought centered around the concept of liberty. People must live in politically organized communities, he believed, and they should be subject only to the minimum amount of control to make such organization possible. Otherwise they should be free. Indeed, for Las Casas, human beings required freedom in order that their reason, which naturally inclined them to live together in peace and harmony, could seek good and avoid evil in an unrestricted manner. If the free exercise of reason constituted a basic human right, it clearly belonged to Native Americans as well as Europeans. Not even the pope, in his enthusiasm to spread the Gospel, might legitimately revoke such a basic human right. Las Casas insisted on free and voluntary conversion even more strongly than any other writer of his time. He simply could not condone the use of force in missionary activity. He also held that the pope, in ordinary circumstances, had no authority whatsoever over non-Christians, and could not punish their sins or overthrow their leaders.

Las Casas considered Native Americans to be subjects of the Spanish government, who, as such, should enjoy all the guarantees of liberty and justice which the Spanish government gave to its native Spanish subjects. They also owed the crown, he felt, the same allegiance and duties as did all Spanish subjects, and Las Casas maintained that Native Americans were just as capable as Spaniards of performing those duties and of receiving the Christian religion. In his ideal missionary empire, the natives would live in their own villages, ruled by their own leaders, under the supervision of Spanish officials who would administer justice, instruct the natives in European customs, and discourage barbarous practices.

Of course, Spanish settlers and conquerors considered Las Casas's ideas to be a serious challenge to their position. No doubt many of these individuals took serious pride in their achievements and thought of themselves as champions of civilization and religion against a cruel and superstitious people. At the theoretical level, these ideas found their greatest defender in Juan Ginés de Sepúlveda, a university professor and one of Spain's leading experts on Aristotle.

Sepúlveda expressed his views in *Democrates Alter*, which he wrote in 1542 at the peak of his career. Basing his case on the theories of Aristotle, Sepúlveda argued that superior races ought to rule inferior ones, and that within each race, the better elements should rule their inferiors. Indeed, Sepúlveda even denied that a people might be considered to have legitimate rulers unless they were governed according to the opinions of the best citizens. For purposes of maintaining peace, however, Sepúlveda expected people to obey even bad leaders, and he disapproved of rebellion against any rulers who had legitimate claims to power according to the particular laws and customs of their society. Aristotle's theories, as Sepúlveda interpreted them, became a mandate for superior races to conquer, by force if necessary, uncivilized peoples and teach them better morals, more honorable customs, and, of course, Christianity. In order that they might learn from missionaries and prepare themselves to become good Christians, Native Americans had be placed under the authority of a Christian government—with or without their consent—for their own good. Civilization and Christianity went hand in hand. Conquest was a religious duty, an act of charity towards an ignorant and unfortunate people.

Sepúlveda's theories produced a storm of protest, especially from Las Casas. Heated discussion of the questions which he had raised continued until 1550, when the government ordered that Sepúlveda and Las Casas debate them before a panel of theologians and lawyers. The proceedings of these debates continued for some time and produced no conclusions. Although the judges reached no decision, it appears that Las Casas won the day. The government wanted to stop the brutal treatment of Native Americans, which had received so much unfavorable publicity. It issued new laws that protected the property and the personal freedom of Native Americans, provided special courts in which Native Americans' grievances could be heard, employed lawyers to defend Native American causes, and instructed judges to enforce native customs and laws where these were not openly barbarous or contrary to Spanish law. Sepúlveda, by the way, never received royal permission to publish his book. *Democrates Alter* only appeared some two hundred years later.

In the course of the sixteenth and seventeenth centuries, America was incorporated into the legal and diplomatic institutions of European civilization. Although it would be an exaggeration to claim that America played a prominent role in European politics, the exploration and conquest of America represented a decisive stage in the spread of European influence around the world. Overseas possessions came to be seen as essential additions to Europe itself, strengthening the military and economic power of its rival nation-states. As European governments took control of new territories, new populations, and new sources of wealth, they inevitably gained confidence in their ability to rule, and in the righteousness of their Christian values. The conquest of Native Americans also raised complex questions about the proper relationship between ruler and subject. The answers to those questions, together with the spread of European political and military might beyond the continent itself, helped shape the course of global politics for centuries to come.

3 / EUROPEAN CONCEPTIONS OF NATIVE AMERICANS

The [Canadian] natives desire nothing but what is necessary to their natural needs, so that they are not gourmets and do not go seek [exotic foods] in distant lands; and their nourishment is healthy, with the result that they do not know what it is to be sick. Rather, they live in continual health and peace and have no occasion to be envious of one another because of their property or patrimony— for they are all almost equal in possessions and are all rich in mutual contentment and degree of poverty. They also have no place designated for administering justice because they do no wrong to each other. They have no laws . . . other than that of nature.

ANDRÉ THEVET
The Singularities of Antarctic France, also called America (1557)

The existence of Native Americans, like that of America itself, was a complete surprise to sixteenth-century Europeans, and the ways in which they came to grips with this new knowledge tell us a good deal about the character and values of their civilization. Explorers' descriptions of various Native American societies stimulated intellectuals at home to reconsider their preconceived notions about such basic concepts as "savage" and "civilized." The new knowledge about these peoples and their communities, moreover, had to be placed within the context of what Europeans already thought about the world and its peoples. Renaissance thought, therefore, played a vital role in determining how and what Europeans thought about Native Americans. Indeed, it provided the basic tools that Europeans needed to investigate the inhabitants of this "new part" of the world.

NATIVE AMERICANS IN EUROPEAN THOUGHT

In European history, serious study of the different peoples and societies around the world began in the Renaissance, when scholars developed a keen interest in the art, culture, and literature of the ancient Greeks and Romans. By studying ancient Greece and Rome, Europeans had unintentionally sharpened their ability to analyze societies elsewhere in the world. The intellectual tools that they developed to analyze the Greek and Roman civilizations, which were separated from their own by time, could also be used to examine Native American civilization, which was separated from Europe by geographical space.

In general, Europeans believed that they might best understand and explain any unfamiliar society by finding out what it had in common with their own. In their attempts to understand these societies, Renaissance scholars focused on the rituals, ceremonies, and behavior patterns that seemed to correspond, more or less, to their own standards of social organization and thought. Generally, these included religion, marriage and family life, burial and mourning customs, methods of warfare, language, clothing, physical appearance, and diet. Yet, by relying closely on such familiar models for their comparisons, Europeans narrowed their vision to such an extent that they found it very difficult to appreciate the distinctive character of the cultures they had encountered.

One good example of the consequences of this narrow vision is the Europeans' evaluation of the different contributions made by women and men to Native American society. They praised native women for their hard work in planting and harvesting crops and gathering herbs and supplies in the wild. Conversely, they condemned the men for being lazy and for amusing themselves by fishing and hunting while contributing little to the maintenance of society. Or so the Europeans thought. In fact, hunting and fishing played a much more important role in the Native American economy than they did in Europe. Europeans failed to understand this difference because they were using their own rigid standards of what constituted "work." They regarded agricultural labor to be the most productive, since it constituted the basic element of the European economy and provided most of the food that Europeans consumed. On the other hand, Europeans thought that hunting and fishing (important sources of food for Native Americans) were merely sports or exercises for native men—amusements for the elite—because they served that function in Europe. Thus, Europeans misjudged the relative importance of male and female contributions to Native American society because they were using inappropriate standards of measurement.

No sixteenth-century account, however, presented a clear and consistent interpretation of Native Americans. Authors often contradicted each other (and themselves). These apparent inconsistencies and contradictions resulted from the difficulties that Europeans experienced in their attempts to explain the unknown in terms of the known, the new in terms of the traditional. No single method of comparison proved comprehensive enough to explain America and its natives, so a number of different concepts had to be used. Not surprisingly, authors faced not only the problem of understanding new knowledge but also of communicating it to the European reading public.

Reconciling their new knowledge about Native Americans with traditional ideas about the various peoples of the world also proved to be a difficult task for scholars. Fortunately, Renaissance culture provided some important intellectual themes which helped in this effort. Perhaps the most useful of these was the myth of a "Golden Age," which contended that sometime in the distant past people had lived long, healthy, untroubled, and simple lives, uncorrupted by civilization. Using this idea, some European authors depicted America as an earthly paradise. They described America as a "lost Eden," with lush forests, multicolored birds, brilliant flowers, and exotic animals. Here natives roamed naked (like Adam and Eve before original sin), and lived in magnificent surroundings. Their longevity, unashamed nakedness, and supposed easy childbirth raised disturbing questions about their need for Christianity and European civilization. Although several authors of early-sixteenth-century travel narratives used this familiar myth as a way to make Native American society comprehensible to their readers, none did so with greater results than Peter Martyr.

Martyr, more than any other individual, gave the European reading public its first impressions of Native Americans. In his *Decades of the New World* (1511), the first published history of the European exploration and conquest of America, he compared the characteristics of life in the Golden Age with that of Native

Americans. Indeed, Martyr emphasized that they lived carefree, healthy, and astonishingly long lives in pleasant surroundings. For Martyr, Native Americans lived in freedom and leisure, without political, legal, or judicial systems, much like Adam and Eve in the Garden of Eden. His assessment, of course, hardly fit the facts, but nevertheless found an enthusiastic reception among Europeans scholars. It influenced many of the interpretations of Native American societies that subsequently appeared in the sixteenth century.

Martyr's great influence over his contemporaries came from the simple fact that he seemed to know more about Native Americans than any other single European. His work contained a wealth of ethnographic and linguistic information about the natives of the newly conquered lands. For example, in 1493, he wrote a letter to Cardinal Ascanio Sforza, which included a vocabulary of words in the Taino language, recorded from the natives of Hispaniola whom Columbus had brought back from his first voyage. This vocabulary is the first European record of any Native American language. Although Martyr was born and educated in Italy, he had moved to Spain in the latter part of the fifteenth century when Queen Isabella, who wanted to upgrade the education of aristocrats' children in Castile, invited him to direct her palace school. As a result of being in Spain at the right time, and moving in the highest political and social circles, Martyr had access to the most up-to-date information about America from Spain's returning explorers. As a man steeped in the classical learning of the Italian Renaissance, he possessed the ability to write it all down in the elegant manner of the educated elite.

European authors also used another, but similar, image of America to make it and its inhabitants more easily understandable to their readers. This explanation centered around the idea that America was, quite literally, a "new land"—created more recently than Europe. Europeans had long speculated on the existence of this land that had survived in the legends of the sunken continent of Atlantis, in tales of mysterious Islands in the Atlantic Ocean, especially the elusive island of Brazil. According to this view, God had created Native Americans more recently than Europeans. Indeed, their rude manners reminded Europeans of their own primitive ancestors.

The idea that Native Americans were living counterparts of European ancestral tribes led to the concept that every race and civilization passed through similar stages of development. The Spanish Jesuit José de Acosta became one of the key figures in the development of this theory (see page 43). While his masterpiece, *The Natural and Moral History of the Indies* (1590), described the unique characteristics of America and its inhabitants, it also emphasized the underlying harmony between European and American civilizations. It established some basic cultural categories for classifying and evaluating different societies. Acosta's approach suggested that all peoples passed through a similar evolutionary process, from a primitive to a civilized state, and he ranked societies in order of their level of development. Acosta delineated three types of primitive societies: the least primitive were those which were literate (the Chinese and Japanese); those in the middle position were characterized by stable governments and organized religions (the Aztecs and Incas); at the bottom were those societies whose inhabitants often lived like wild beasts (the Caribbean natives). With this scheme, Acosta depicted an evolutionary process from savagery through two degrees of barbarism to civilization—defined, of course, according to European values and beliefs. Acosta obviously believed in the benefits of studying a wide variety of societies, no matter how backward, because such an investigation would give Europeans significant insights into the evolution of their own cultural condition. These lesser-developed societies supposedly served as living examples of what Europeans had been like ages ago.

In the process of inventing this hierarchy of societies, Acosta raised a question that had perplexed and fascinated Europeans for a long time: why did these differences among peoples and societies exist in the first place? For Renaissance Europeans, the customary answer emphasized the consequences of living in different climates. Acosta's observations of Native Americans, however, focused attention on alternative explanations, especially the importance of the migrations of peoples. Acosta, who argued that Native Americans came to America over a land bridge from Asia, believed that they had changed from farmers into hunters during their migration. Then, gradually, some Native Americans gathered together in certain regions of America and began to organize themselves socially and politically.

In France, the work of the historian La Popelinière echoed Acosta's and also illuminated the ways in which Renaissance intellectuals responded to the problems involved in confronting strange cultures. His *The Three Worlds* (1582) shows how the expanding horizons of the sixteenth century broadened the scope of the historian. Unlike many of his contemporaries, La Popelinière had no interest in an encyclopedic collection of cultural information for its own sake; he sought a more profound understanding of the development of historical thought and of the historical process itself.

La Popelinière did not want merely to point out similarities and differences between European and American customs; he wanted to explain their origins. He believed that knowledge of different societies at different stages of development might tell Europeans something important about their own historical development. In other words, through observation of primitive societies, Europeans could better understand their own beginnings. For La Popelinière, savages represented the living past. He did not question their humanity, since savagery for him represented only a temporary condition that could—and would—be outgrown. He thought that knowledge of other cultures helped people understand how societies, and the idea of history itself, developed. One could now study other cultures in their various stages, thanks to the voyages of exploration, and see how each stage represented a different method of recording a people's history.

These theories about the development of human society had important implications for Europeans' ideas about the historical process. Comparisons of native societies with those of the European past revealed some striking similarities, suggesting that the ancestors of modern Europeans had once lived like the present inhabitants of America. The history of art provides a good example of this development. The drawings of North American natives in 1585 by the English artist John White served as the basis for imaginative illustrations of ancient Picts and Britons. By the end of the sixteenth century, then, the experience of America had provided Europeans with the outlines of a theory of social and cultural development.

Although many of the early assessments of Native Americans followed Martyr's influential "Golden Age" analogy, more negative assessments began to appear as the sixteenth century progressed. Historians differ about why this happened. Some believe that the changed perceptions of Native Americans resulted from more frequent contact with North American natives, whose societies impressed Europeans less favorably than those of the Aztecs or Incas, while others emphasize the increasingly pessimistic outlook towards virtually all aspects of human society that accompanied the gradual transition from Renaissance to Reformation Europe.

According to this more negative view, Native Americans lived in a world dominated by Satan. Here nature ran wild, and people were almost unbelievably savage and evil. They practiced cannibalism and devil-worship, had disgusting personal habits, and, especially, refused to recognize Christianity as the one true religion. In general, advocates of this point of view regarded Native Americans as little better than animals, incapable of reasoning or adapting to European customs—in fact, fit only to serve their European masters.

Such advocates felt they found plenty of evidence to support their opinions. One English eyewitness, for example, said that Native Americans he saw in London in 1501 wore animal skins, ate raw flesh, and had the manners of savage beasts. Another eyewitness in Lisbon, at about the same time, mentioned that Native Americans were "well-formed" physically, but in reality his descriptions of them emphasized the tattoos on their faces and bodies (which he found repulsive) and their "bestial" manners and habits. He said they were like "wild men." In fact, no feature of Native American life interested Europeans more than cannibalism. Authors often described it in gruesome detail. In one of his published letters, for example, Amerigo Vespucci claimed that he met a Native American who boasted of having eaten more than three hundred human beings, and Vespucci claimed that he saw preserved human flesh hanging, like pork, from the beams of their houses.

Stimulated by these grisly descriptions, Renaissance thinkers turned to an old legend to help them understand Native Americans. The so-called hairy wild man was a familiar character in medieval folklore, art, and mythology. With a combination of animal and human traits, the wild man epitomized a human being who had degenerated into a beast. To Renaissance thinkers, he represented a hideous creature, wearing no clothes and covered with a thick coat of hair or fur. Passion guided his life; he was notorious for his uncontrollable lust. The wild man provided a familiar context within which the strange and unknown natives might be more easily comprehended by Europeans. Indeed, many travelers to America anticipated that Native Americans would resemble this half-human, half-bestial creature. The existence of this preconceived image of savage life encouraged travelers to America to expect the worst from Native Americans—and with these expectations in mind, travelers naturally underestimated the amount of social and political organization in their societies.

Most sixteenth-century Europeans considered the Tupinamba of Brazil, who wore no clothes and practiced cannibalism, to be living examples of these wild men. Indeed, the Frenchman André Thevet, who lived in Brazil briefly in the mid-1550s, provided the classic definition of savagery when he described the Tupinamba as lacking Christianity, kings, and laws. None of these interpretations, of course, provided a true description. The Tupinamba did practice cannibalism, but their society also had a social and political framework that almost completely eluded European observers. Instead, Europeans had come to these blatantly erroneous conclusions because they misunderstood native society, which they viewed only in comparison to their own rather than on its own terms.

In addition to an overriding belief in the superiority of their own culture, Europeans' inability to understand Native American languages contributed to their habit of oversimplifying Native American societies. Although European travelers attempted to master Native American languages, and sometimes included dictionaries and phrasebooks of native speech in their accounts to help in that effort, as in the case of Peter Martyr, they usually failed in their attempts to fully understand them. As a result, Europeans dismissed Native American languages as inferior because they lacked the ability to express abstract concepts. Moreover, they broadened this highly subjective judgment to include Native Americans' general intellectual development.

To Europeans, Native Americans (like animals) appeared to be concerned only with those aspects of the tangible world that they could perceive through the senses. Despite the alleged poverty of Native American languages, however, Europeans optimistically believed that this linguistic and mental deficiency could be remedied through proper education.

European attitudes towards Native Americans depended, to a considerable extent, on biblical theories about origins. In the Renaissance, virtually all Europeans accepted without question the account of creation contained in the Old Testament. They believed that the various peoples of the world descended from Noah's sons: Asians from Shem, Africans from Ham, and Europeans from Japhet. The encounter with Native Americans, however, raised new and significant questions for Europeans. Where did Native Americans come from? How did they fit into the biblical account of creation? No doubt the most curious answer to this problem came from the Swiss physician Paracelsus. Around 1520, he asserted that Native Americans did not descend from the same Adam and Eve as the rest of humanity. Instead, he thought they came from a completely different "Adam and Eve," and that God had created them sometime after the great flood described in the Old Testament.

The theories of other thinkers seem less bizarre. The Frenchman Urbain Chauveton, for example, like Acosta, speculated that Native Americans had migrated to America from Asia over a narrow landbridge which separated the two continents. He based his theory on similarities that he perceived in the cultural and political organization of Native Americans and Asians. Others made efforts to identify Native Americans with the ten lost tribes of Israel, or as descendants of the original inhabitants of the sunken continent of Atlantis. Although the question of the natives' origin found no definitive answer in the Renaissance, the debate led Europeans to downplay the idea that humanity was uniform.

The belief that Native Americans lacked culture remained remarkably persistent in the sixteenth century. To a large extent, Europeans based this conclusion on their low opinion of Native American religion. They thought that this, more than any other single factor, indicated the level of a society's development—and in this area they simply would not tolerate diversity. The fact that Native Americans apparently had no knowledge of Christianity bothered Europeans; their paganism clearly indicated their inferiority. Europeans found it difficult to even categorize the religious status of Native Americans. They failed to find such familiar external signs of organized religion as churches, prayers, written creeds, religious symbols, or holidays. As a result, Europeans decided that Native Americans had no religion at all. This troubling conclusion raised a number of tricky questions: did Native Americans have souls? were they capable of becoming Christians? could they be saved? were they fully human? These questions puzzled and profoundly disturbed Europeans. If Native Americans were not fully human, what was their proper place among life on earth? Were they, as some argued, natural slaves? Could their status ever be improved? The answers to these questions were important, because they determined the kind of treatment Native Americans might expect from their European conquerors.

The debate about the status and nature of Native Americans began with the purely practical issue of how the Spanish government ought to administer its American possessions. The Spanish government chose to base its policies on the feudal system, treating settlers as "lords" who received grants of land, with native "serfs" to do the actual work. This idea seemed to lead to disaster: Native Americans soon began to die in large numbers. Although modern historians have traced the cause of their near-annihilation to the natives' inability to resist germs and infections imported from Europe, in the sixteenth century many observers attributed it to the cruelty of the Spanish masters (the so-called Black Legend). To save the natives from further abuse and exploitation, Queen Isabella issued a royal decree in 1503 restricting enslavement to "a certain people called Cannibals." Spaniards, however, interpreted this broadly as a license to enslave any natives suspected of cannibalism from any of the Caribbean islands. When they proved to be unsatisfactory laborers, Spaniards imported African slaves in ever increasing numbers starting in 1518.

The debate about the status and character of Native Americans continued throughout the sixteenth century. In 1525, the Dominican Tomas Ortiz gave a speech in which he outlined the argument supporting the enslavement of Native Americans. He repeated the charges that their societies lacked judicial or administrative systems and that the natives themselves could not be educated. Moreover, he found despicable their personal habits such as eating raw fleas, spiders, and worms. These defects, he asserted (following the theories of Aristotle), justified the European enslavement of Native Americans on the grounds that it would improve the Native American ways of life. Other Spaniards repeated this hypothesis throughout the century. For example, in 1558, Pedro de Grante compared Native Americans with wild animals because both lacked the ability to think rationally. On the whole, Spaniards and other Europeans tended to regard Native Americans as children or inferior beings, capable only of serving, and learning from, Europeans. Indeed, the Spanish government recognized its obligation to protect the natives and established a committee to study the issue. In 1512, the Laws of Burgos officially defined the status of Native Americans, placing them under the government's protection.

Although the Laws of Burgos provided a framework for a rational Spanish policy towards Native Americans, they did not answer any of the legal and administrative problems posed by the very existence of Native Americans in the first place. Therefore, Spaniards reverted to traditional European conventions. For example, in 1513 King Ferdinand issued a decree prohibiting Spaniards from conquering Native Americans unless the natives failed to respond to a document formally read to them in front of witnesses. This document demanded that Native Americans recognize the fact that Pope Alexander VI had given these "new" lands to Ferdinand and Isabella and also that they should acknowledge the Catholic Church (and, by implication, the Pope) as the legitimate ruler of the world. The document also warned that if the natives should resist, they were to be treated as rebels. Thus, the Spanish government treated America, from a legal point of view, as a remote province of Spain.

This document also demonstrates that Spaniards occupied the Caribbean islands and the American mainland in the name of the church as well as the state. Missionaries, who began to arrive in 1502, enjoyed little success in converting the natives, attributing their failures to exaggerated tales of Spanish cruelty towards Native Americans. As long as Spanish settlers continued to abuse Native Americans, missionaries could hardly expect to make many converts. Accordingly, they appealed to Ferdinand and Isabella to protect their new subjects. Their appeal took on a wider significance, moreover, because it raised questions about whether Native Americans could be regarded as bona fide subjects of the crown and members of the church.

Renaissance intellectuals believed that God had set human beings apart from the rest of creation by giving them souls, allowing them to receive divine grace, and giving them the power to think rationally. Many of the first European settlers in America firmly believed that Native Americans failed to demonstrate any of these hallmarks of humanity. In 1517, one member of the Spanish royal council declared that Native Americans were so low on the scale of humanity that they were incapable of receiving the faith; in 1528, a Dominican, Domingo de Betanzos, said that their savagery condemned Native Americans to a rapid and well-deserved extinction. He even refused to regard them as human beings because, he said, they ate human flesh and practiced sodomy, had no sense of justice, understood no teaching, and openly rejected Christianity.

When it became clear that appeals to the Spanish government to protect Native Americans had little effect, reform-minded Spaniards asked the Pope to intercede. In one reform effort during 1535, the bishop of Tlaxcala, in Mexico, wrote to Pope Paul III, praising the intelligence of Native Americans. He even blamed the devil for causing Europeans to believe that Native Americans could not understand the doctrines of Christianity. Two years later, a Dominican missionary who had worked in Mexico and Nicaragua, Bernadino da Minaya, went to Rome to plead the case of Native Americans in person. As a result of these efforts, in 1537 Pope Paul III officially declared Native Americans to be "true men," capable of receiving the Catholic faith. He warned Christians not to treat Native Americans as "dumb brutes created for our service," or to deprive them of their property or personal freedom by any means. After this proclamation, Europeans generally accepted that American natives were human, but the exact degree of their humanity remained a matter of debate. Fernández de Oviedo, for instance, claimed to have found evidence of their natural inferiority, idleness, and inclination towards vice in the thickness of their skulls. A deformity in that part of the body, he believed, provided a true indication of a person's limited potential for rational thought.

While discussion raged around the status of Native Americans, many Europeans had opportunities to observe them in person. Columbus had taken some natives back to Spain with him after his first voyage to America in 1492, and the explorers who led later expeditions followed his example. In those early years, however, most Europeans regarded Native Americans as mere savages, living somewhere on the edge of Asia and therefore not much different from the Asians with whom Europeans had long been familiar. As a result, the Native Americans aroused relatively little attention. In 1525, for example, word spread among the population of Coruña that a ship had arrived carrying a cargo of cloves (*clavos*), but their high hopes turned to disappointment with the discovery that it brought nothing more glamorous than slaves (*esclavos*), illegally captured in North America. Port officials promptly released the slaves.

Mexicans brought to Spain in 1528 by Hernándo Cortés aroused much more curiosity. In addition to being inhabitants of a "New World" now known to be distinct from Asia, they also represented the Aztec empire, which was exciting the imaginations of many Europeans who had heard tales of its wealth, sophistication, and grandeur. Christoph Weiditz, a German artist, who saw these jugglers and "ballplayers" perform before King Charles in Toledo, executed a fascinating series of drawings which bring them vividly to life. Cortés sent some of these Mexicans to Rome in 1529, where they "juggled a log with their feet" before a delighted Pope Clement VII, who thanked God that such peoples had been discovered during his lifetime.

Most Europeans, however, derived their impressions from more primitive Native American societies than the Aztecs. As we have seen, a few natives from Newfoundland arrived in Portugal in 1501 and England in the following year. Others from Cape Breton reached France in 1508. In 1505, Binot Palmier de Gonneville brought a feared Brazilian native named Essomericq, the son of a chief, to Spain. This Native American converted to Christianity and even married one of Gonneville's daughters. William Hawkins, returning to England from a South

American voyage in 1532, presented a Brazilian chief to King Henry VIII. According to one account of this encounter, Henry and his nobles marveled at the fact that this person had small bones set in his cheeks and a precious stone, "about the size of a pea," in his lower lip.

When the French king Henry II, together with his queen, Catherine de Medici, and other aristocrats, visited Rouen in 1550, the local businessmen took the opportunity to lobby the government on behalf of their trade in dyewood with Brazil. They recreated a Tupinamba village, where some fifty natives (together with native Frenchmen disguised as Native Americans) danced, fought staged battles with each other, shot at birds with bows and arrows, climbed trees, and paddled canoes. An illustrated book published to commemorate the king's visit described the scene. When, in 1555, the French established a colony in Brazil (at the site of modern-day Rio de Janeiro), they brought even more natives to France. Some of these took part in several of the entertainments devised for King Charles IX when he made state visits to provincial capitals—in Rouen in 1563, in Troyes in 1564, and at Bordeaux in 1565.

Partly as a result of French efforts to settle colonists in Brazil, Europeans became more familiar with the native Tupinambas than with any other Native Americans in the sixteenth century. Indeed, they inspired three famous travel books. A German mercenary soldier, Hans Staden, who fought for the Portuguese government in Brazil wrote the first and probably the most interesting. His *Truthful History and Description of the Landscape of the Wild, Naked, Cruel, Man-Eating People in the New World of America* (1557) became a bestseller. Written in a lively, personal manner, with woodcut illustrations based on his own drawings, it provided a wealth of information about the Tupinamba as they existed at the moment they first came into contact with Europeans. Among other things, Staden described their religious beliefs, marriage customs, agricultural methods, and the ways in which they decorated their naked bodies with pigments, shells, stones, and feathers. Primarily, however, Staden wanted to record how God had saved him after these cannibals had taken him prisoner. He vividly described how his captors stripped him naked and led him to their village, forcing him to announce his arrival by crying out: "Here I come, food for you." Indeed, cannibalism is one of the main subjects of the book, and Staden recorded its ceremonies and rituals in gruesome detail. On one occasion, he boldly criticized their great chief Quoniambec, who was gnawing on a human leg, by telling him that even wild beasts do not eat each other. The chief, according to Staden, replied that he was like a jaguar and that the flesh tasted good.

André Thevet's *The Singularities of Antarctic France, also called America* (1557) provided an equally unappealing picture of the same tribe. This popular book played an important part in forming the French impression of the Tupinamba. The Native Americans' nakedness shocked this Franciscan friar, and he concluded that Native Americans lived like unreasonable beasts. The Protestant Jean de Léry, however, had a more tolerant opinion of Tupinamba nakedness in his *History of a Voyage to the Land of Brésil* (1578). He compared the innocent nakedness of Tupinamba women favorably with the habits of Parisian women, who wore elaborate clothes and jewels specifically to attract members of the opposite sex. In England, George Best also found himself favorably impressed by the social graces of Native Americans—in this case, a male and female Eskimo brought back from Baffin Island to England by Martin Frobisher in 1576. He appears to have been especially impressed by the couple's modesty and discrete sexual behavior.

New knowledge gained from the exploits of explorers in the Renaissance would have merely provided some amusement and satisfied the curiosity of relatively few Europeans if not for printing. Letters and pamphlets announcing news of the latest expeditions and the great collections of travel literature by Gian Battista Ramusio and Richard Hakluyt brought into existence an impressive written record of Europe's overseas expansion. These collections of travel literature spread new information about America to the European reading public, and profoundly altered the ways in which some intellectuals thought about the character and history of their world.

Yet, it remains difficult to measure the amount of interest in America by the number of books published about it in the six-teenth century. Only a small percentage of Renaissance books seem to have been devoted to travel and geography in the first place; and of these, works on America clearly constituted a minority. Modern scholars, for example, have estimated that in France between 1480 and 1609 twice as many books and ten times as many pamphlets were devoted to the Middle East than to the Americas. Moreover, if we exclude from this list works which either describe America as a part of Asia (almost all publications before the 1520s) or record attempts to reach Asia by way of America, these figures would be reduced even further.

Statistics can be misleading. The ratio between the number of books published and their influence on the people who read them can never be established with any degree of certainty for the sixteenth century (or any other time), and historians know virtually nothing about the other ways of spreading information. For example, the sixteenth-century Spaniard Luis de Matos said that people talked about the "New World" everywhere in Europe, yet historians today remain totally ignorant about the extent and content of these conversations. Nevertheless, a good number of writers such as the Spanish historian Francisco López de Gómara (see page 23) clearly grasped the significance of the "New World."

No sixteenth-century book did more to inform Europeans about America than the collection of travel literature which Gian Battista Ramusio published in Venice in the 1550s. His three-volume collection of *Voyages and Travels* was truly international in its sources and worldwide in its scope. Ramusio's interest in collecting accounts of European explorations derived in no small part from a desire to compare what the ancient Greeks and Romans knew about the rest of world with the theories of his own day. He translated ancient Greek accounts of navigation between Africa and India and compared their information on spices and winds with that in accounts he had of the Portuguese voyages. He took delight in the enormous progress during his lifetime in geographical knowledge. His work gave wide circulation to Jacques Cartier's account of his voyages down the St. Lawrence River (to the site of present-day Montreal), and he also printed the first account of John Cabot's voyage to Newfoundland in 1497. In his third volume (1556), Ramusio became the first to publish Giovanni da Verrazzano's account of his exploration of the American coast from Cape Fear to Newfoundland in 1524.

The second great compiler of travel literature was the Englishman Richard Hakluyt. Living in Paris in the early 1580s, it aggravated him to hear the French praise other nations for their overseas activities but ignore English efforts. To correct this situation, he published *Divers Voyages, touching the discoverie of America and the Ilands adjacent unto the same* in 1582, and *Principal Navigations, Voyages & Discoveries of the English Nation* in 1589. The latter, the "prose epic of the English nation," is perhaps the most important historical work of the century. Hakluyt's work provided a complete collection of English travels and commerce—it still serves as the indispensable source for the study of English voyages in the Age of Exploration. After Hakluyt's death in 1616, Samuel Purchas continued this great work in *Purchas His Pilgrimes.*

Not only more complete than any that had preceded them, the English collections of Hakluyt and Purchas also had a specific purpose: to lobby for a greater English presence overseas. Indeed, Hakluyt's activity took place on the eve of the formation of the East India Company and the settlement of Jamestown. He had great enthusiasm for the possibilities of a future British empire, emphasizing two areas especially: eastern North America and India. He wrote a plea for American colonization in *Discourse on the Western Planting*, which circulated in manuscript long before its publication in 1877. Yet the *Principal Navigations* remains Hakluyt's masterpiece. Throughout the 1590s he edited, expanded, and updated this collection of travel literature (the first edition contained some seventy thousand words, the second edition about one million, seven hundred thousand). Together with this work, Hakluyt also translated important eyewitness accounts of America, a project of almost equal importance.

The De Bry family in Frankfurt published another collection of travel literature which had a long-lasting influence on European perceptions of America between 1590 and 1634. Like Hakluyt's work, the De Bry publishers designed this collection to make a political point as well as convey information. Without exception, the Protestant De Brys selected authors who were hostile to Catholic Spain. Thus, on page after page, cruel Spaniards confront noble natives, with the point of the narrative reinforced by several fascinating illustrations (Ramusio's volumes had a few woodcuts and Hakluyt's none). The De Bry pictures depict the conflict between the Protestant English and Native Americans in the North quite differently: here, the English are heroes and the natives are villains—with the exception of Pocahontas, who married an Englishman.

In addition to travel accounts and histories, the European exploration and conquest of America also influenced other types of literature. One of the first, and most famous, examples of this impact is Thomas More's classic, *Utopia* (1516). It shows the author's enthusiasm about America, as well as the impact of the "discovery" in intellectual circles. More understood very well the significance of the "New World"; his brother-in-law, John Rastell, who had traveled there, wrote a lengthy poem based on his experience (*The Interlude of the Four Elements*), which contained the first English description of America. More also knew about other travel accounts, especially those of Amerigo Vespucci, who had portrayed Native Americans as living in a Golden Age, leading idyllic lives and possessing no private property.

Without a doubt, *Utopia* reflects More's knowledge about the voyages of exploration. The story's narrator, Raphael Hythloday, claimed that he had made three visits to Utopia while accompanying Vespucci on his expeditions to America, and More placed his ideal society on an island in the South Atlantic. Obviously, America appealed to More as a pure and uncorrupted locale, well-suited for the establishment of an ideal community: it provided the model for "utopian" society. More's work shows us that for many Europeans, America represented, above all, a place where human beings could live in freedom, liberated from the traditional constraints of European life. Indeed, More created this fictional society to serve as a means by which to condemn European social and political practices. For More, this "New World" clearly offered possibilities for improving society that could not be found in Europe.

More clearly regarded the European society of his time with disgust. To him, poverty, injustice, war, hatred, and political strife had only served to spread misfortune everywhere. In *Utopia*, More has Hythloday confirm what Columbus and Vespucci had already announced—that another world existed where people lived much more satisfying lives. His conclusion followed inevitably: Europeans had, in many ways, departed from the true path, and as a consequence, they had been condemned to live miserable lives. Yet, More made no specific references to Native Americans in his work. His main theme provided Europeans with a model of an ideal life and society to which they might aspire. Consequently, More did not directly speculate regarding the nature of Native Americans and their culture.

Many authors in addition to More fantasized about ideal societies. Other European writers who described such societies often placed them in the "New World" but populated them exclusively with Europeans. Nor were they always mere fantasies. Sir Humphrey Gilbert—who had read *Utopia*—drew up detailed plans for a colony which he hoped to establish in America. He envisioned it ruled by a governor with an elected council, with free housing provided for poor immigrants and land set aside to support a hospital and schools: all the colonists would enjoy the political rights of freeborn Englishmen. One historian of his voyages complacently remarked that it seemed as if God had reserved North America for the English.

In France, the poet Etienne Jodelle compared the French unfavorably to the natives of Brazil in order to criticize the hypocrisy of civilized nations. He asserted that Europeans were no less barbarous than Native Americans; although the French were more rational than Native Americans, they used their rationality for evil purposes. Like Léry, he regarded the nakedness of Native Americans as no more offensive than the artificial ornaments Europeans used to alter their appearance. In a similar manner, Pierre de Ronsard's *Complaint Against Fortune* (1559) depicted the natives of Brazil as living representatives of the blissful existence idealized by ancient Greek and Roman poets. He described Native Americans as living happily, without any suffering or anxiety, holding all of their possessions in common. He also questioned the desirability of a French presence in America, insisting that Europeans would most likely only corrupt the purity of Native Americans.

In two of his essays, *Des Cannibals* (1580) and *Des Coches* (1588), Michel de Montaigne used images of the Native American as a vehicle to express his ideas about life in a state of nature. *Des Cannibals*, Montaigne's best-known essay on Native Americans, idealized their lives as simple, virtuous, and uncorrupted. He praised their manner of life as guided by the laws of nature and compared it unfavorably with the artificial, and often violent, characteristics of European civilized society. In *Des Coches*, Montaigne argued that Native Americans were rational and equal to Europeans in most respects. Indeed, he found their cities of Cusco and Mexico to have an "astounding magnificence."

Above all, however, Montaigne popularized the idea of the "Noble Savage." In so doing, he transformed the myth of the Golden Age from a literary theme to a way of interpreting the societies of real people. He compared the "primitive Indian" with the sophisticated European, however, not so much to praise the former as to scold his fellow Europeans for their corruption, moral indifference, and hypocrisy. In this way, he hoped to provoke reform of some of the worst abuses of contemporary society. For him, the existence of America not only revealed living examples of naturally virtuous peoples, it heightened awareness of the great variety of human societies and customs. In fact, *Des Cannibals* is nothing less than an attempt to define what the term "civilized" meant. In the process, Montaigne provided an American location for the "good savage" of classical literature, using him as a vehicle for satirizing the materialistic and shallow European society that he saw around him.

Evidently, Shakespeare had read Montaigne's essays in John Florio's English translation of 1603. He shared Montaigne's interest in America and in the question of what happens when civilization and savagery collide. In *The Tempest*, first performed in 1611, Shakespeare used the relationship between the savage Caliban and the civilized Prospero to raise this issue. In the character of Caliban (whose name is an anagram of the word cannibal), Shakespeare presented an American "savage," far different from Montaigne's "Noble Savage." Caliban, who is brutal and fierce, represented a rather negative assessment of the natives' character. Shakespeare himself obviously esteemed the arts and the other refinements of civilization, depicted by Prospero, above the natural condition of man, represented by Caliban. He believed that savages should not be left in their natural condition but should be elevated to a higher level of human development through education. On the other hand,

Shakespeare seems to be suggesting that even a temporary return to nature helps to make the civilized person even more civilized. Thus, the existence of Native Americans prompted him, like Montaigne and other thinkers of the time, to reconsider the benefits and liabilities of civilization. Shakespeare's debt to Montaigne in *The Tempest* is also demonstrated by the character of Gonzalo, who closely paraphrases Montaigne's thoughts on America when describing the commonwealth Gonzalo would create if he had the chance:

> I' th' commwealth I would by contraries
> Execute all things; for no kind of traffic
> Would I admit; no name of magistrate;
> Letters should not be known; riches, poverty,
> And use of service, none; contract, succession,
> Bourne, bound of land, tilth, vineyard, none;
> No use of metal, corn, or wine, or oil;
> No occupation; all men idle, all;
> And women too, but innocent and pure:
> No sovereignty—
> All things in common nature should produce
> Without sweat or endeavour. Treason, felony,
> Sword, pike, knife, gun, or need of any engine,
> Would I not have; but nature should bring forth,
> Of its own kind, all foison [plenty], all abundance,
> To feed my innocent people. . . .
> I would with such perfection govern, sir,
> T'excell the Golden Age." (act II, scene I)

Although Shakespeare probably had no intention of making *The Tempest* into a symbol of the English colonial experience, the play touches on many of the problems that confronted the members of the Virginia Company. For example, the lustful Caliban, who is so helpful to Prospero at the beginning of their relationship, eventually turns treacherous, in much the same manner as Thomas Hariot stated the natives did to the English settlers at the first Virginia colony. Native Americans' "Golden Age" virtues could turn against Englishmen, as John Smith related in his *Generall Historie of Virginia* (1624): "We chanced in a land even as God made it, where we found only an idle, improvident, scattered people, ignorant of the knowledge of gold and silver, or any commodities, and careless of anything but from hand to mouth, except baubles of no worth." In England, as in France, this image coexisted with that of the handsome, simple, and naturally virtuous savage.

NATIVE AMERICANS IN EUROPEAN ART

In 1520, the great German artist Albrecht Dürer saw some of the Aztec treasure that the Spaniards had stolen from Mexico. He said that its beauty simply astounded him. Before they shipped it to Europe, Spaniards in Mexico compiled an inventory of what they had taken: their list included one hundred ounces of gold ore, a large alligator's head modeled in gold, shields covered with plates of gold, and what Dürer, himself, described as a large wheel, made of gold, with figures of strange animals, weighing 3,800 ounces (probably an Aztec calendar). He found other objects decorated with the plumage of colorful birds or pieces of embroidered cotton.

Yet, despite their splendor, Aztec works of art failed to have any significant effect on the development of European art in the Renaissance. The classical past still exercised a much greater influence over artists than did the "New World." Nevertheless, exotic objects from America, as well as the very existence of Native Americans themselves, did stimulate the interest of some Europeans. Their responses to American artifacts, however limited, significantly reveal which features of America appealed to the European imagination.

Although Europe's great artists appear to have been little influenced by the existence of America or its inhabitants, other Europeans found themselves fascinated by various objects and artifacts of these previously unknown societies. As a result, a number of items brought to Europe from America found their way into the hands of collectors seeking additions to their "cabinets of curiosities." Popular in the Renaissance, these "cabinets" usually contained exotic objects collected from all over the world. A typical list of their contents might include such wonders as ostrich eggs, pieces of quartz, dried flowers, stuffed birds and reptiles, Egyptian idols, Chinese porcelain, Japanese lacquer, and tiny carvings in wood or ivory. To these items collectors eagerly added the wonders of America—hammocks, canoes,

Brazilian clubs and rattles, Mexican featherwork, stone carvings, and ancient manuscripts that described how Native Americans lived, worked, and worshipped.

To a large extent, collecting curiosities became a hobby of the political and social elite. Some of the more successful collectors included the Holy Roman Emperors Ferdinand I (the younger brother of Charles V) and Rudolph II, Duke Albert V of Bavaria, and members of the Medici family in Florence. By 1539, for example, the Medici ruler of Florence had assembled some forty-four pieces of featherwork, including various garments, and by 1553 he owned several wooden masks covered with turquoise and animal heads carved out of semiprecious stones. The passion for collecting, however, quickly spread to other segments of society. Before the end of the sixteenth century, private citizens had begun to form their own cabinets of curiosities that included Native American artifacts. In Bologna, the Italian naturalist Ulisse Aldrovandi built one of the most notable collections, including a turquoise-encrusted Mexican mask, a Mexican knife with an obsidian blade, and a Brazilian axe. In England, John Dee, Queen Elizabeth's astrologer, owned a Mexican obsidian disc, which he is supposed to have used to conjure up spirits—he called it "the Devil's looking-glass." Walter Cope, a London merchant who had traveled to the West Indies, had several specimens of American and other foreign artifacts in his house. A German traveler, Thomas Plater, visited him in 1599 and noted that in addition to Chinese porcelain and Roman coins, Cope owned some beautiful plumes, a stone axe, a Madonna made of feathers, two beautifully dyed sheepskins, and a long, narrow canoe.

As these collections demonstrate, Europeans had a keen interest in Native American artifacts, but they especially prized the natural products of America: pearls, precious stones, gold and silver (of course), and, especially, the colorful plumage of exotic birds. Europeans admired both the beauty of the plumes and the patterns and pictures that native craftsmen made with them. From the very beginning, brightly colored birds played a prominent part in the European image of America. Columbus mentioned them in his first letter reporting the results of his voyage to Ferdinand and Isabella, and he brought some specimens back to Europe with him in 1493. Indeed, in the early

1500s, explorers' reports often referred to Brazil as the "land of parrots." Appropriately, therefore, examples of native feather-work represented America in these collections of curiosities; not surprisingly, illustrations of Native American women wearing nothing but toucan feathers appeared throughout Aldrovandi's book on ornithology.

Of all living creatures, the birds of the West Indies and South America most impressed the early explorers, and with good reason. The parrots particularly appealed to them, because they were both larger and more colorful than the African species already prized in Europe. Indeed, a number of early-sixteenth-century maps included brightly colored birds, with orange-red, yellow, and green plumage, to characterize the fauna of South America. Within a short time, parrots began to appear prominently in Renaissance painting. The Venetian artist Vittore Carpaccio placed a large parrot in the center of one of his pictures of the legend of St. George, while hummingbirds and Mexican quails appear in paintings in the Vatican. Renaissance artists probably became familiar with parrots and other American birds by seeing the stuffed specimens of the more colorful South American birds that sailors brought back to Europe, and Pierre Belon described and illustrated three of them, including a toucan and a macaw, in his pioneering study of ornithology of 1555. The Grand Duke of Tuscany, however, settled neither for paintings of birds nor stuffed specimens. His private aviary included live macaws and curassows, which were depicted in exquisite watercolors by the artist Jacopo Ligozzi, who supplied copies to Aldrovandi.

In addition to these collections of Native American artifacts and American objects, European artists also produced portraits of individual Native Americans and scenes of their life, drawn from first-hand experience. The Frenchman Jacques Le Moyne, who visited Florida in the 1560s, and the Englishman John White, who lived in North America in the 1580s, appeared to be the most important and influential artists to depict native life. These two artists produced the first, and the most complete, visual record of the lives of North American natives in the sixteenth century.

The French explorer René de Laudonnière took Jacques Le Moyne with him to Florida in the 1560s because he wanted

Le Moyne to paint what he saw. Unfortunately, only one of Le Moyne's original American paintings survives, and most of what we know about Le Moyne's observations about Florida and its sixteenth-century inhabitants comes from watercolor copies by White and engravings later published by Theodore de Bry, who altered and "improved" the originals. The faces and figures in these later prints are unmistakably European, despite their hair styles and painted ornaments. Le Moyne's work showed how the French arrived on the coast of Florida, explored the rivers, and built a fort on an island in one of them. He also illustrated the daily life of the inhabitants, at peace and at war: how they took advice from a sorcerer before starting a military campaign, how they declared war, marched to battle, dismembered and scalped the dead, and celebrated their victories to the sound of rattles and drums. He also devoted other scenes to their methods of cooking food, the administration of justice, and religious ceremonies, including the sacrifice of firstborn children to the chief. In the text accompanying his engravings, Le Moyne described such peculiar subjects as hunting alligators:

> Near the river they put up a little hut full of cracks and holes. In this hut one of their men keeps watch. From his hiding place he can see and hear the animals, even if they are a long way off. Then the alligators, driven to the shore by hunger, give themselves away by their loud bellowing, which can be heard at a great distance.
>
> The watchman in the hut now calls his companions, who are waiting in readiness, and they set out for the hunt. They take with them a ten-foot pointed pole, and when they come upon the monster—who usually crawls along with open mouth, ready to attack—they push the pole quickly down its throat. The rough tree bark of its sides prevents the pole from slipping out again.
>
> Then the beast is turned over on its back and killed by beating it with clubs and piercing its soft belly with arrows. The alligators are such a menace that a regular watch has to be kept against them day and night. The Indians guard themselves against these animals just as we guard ourselves from our most dangerous enemies.[1]

---

1 Cited in *The New World: The First Pictures of America*, ed. Stefan Lorant (New York: Duell, Sloan & Pierce, 1946), 87.

John White's drawings are far more realistic than de Bry's engravings of Le Moyne's work. Perhaps because White had a personal interest in the success of the first Virginia colony (he became its governor in 1587), he gives a distinctly favorable impression of Native American life. White avoided showing some of the more disagreeable aspects of Native American life—one would never suspect from his drawings, for example, that when he returned to the colony in 1590, he found no survivors. In this respect, White is a less honest observer than Le Moyne, concentrating on innocent scenes, showing natives sitting around the village fire or participating in various rituals and dances. White also concerned himself with demonstrating that the natives of Virginia wore clothing, contrary to common reports of the natives' shameless nudity. Even the medicine men wore animal skins covering their sex organs, and young native women covered their breasts as a token of their modesty.

Theodore de Bry, who published and illustrated a large number of travel accounts, also provided an idealized view of Native Americans. His motivation, at least in part, originated in a desire to criticize Spanish treatment of Native Americans and fuel the so-called Black Legend of Spanish atrocities towards Native Americans, as we have seen. His multivolume work, aptly titled *America*, contained nothing written by a Spaniard, and largely served to point out the contrasts between peaceloving and gentle Native Americans on the one hand, and the cruel (and Catholic) Spaniards on the other. Artistic considerations, however, played a major role in his work. At a time when the only accepted models for the depiction of the naked human form were antique statues, De Bry's artists promoted and spread the belief that Native Americans were barely distinguishable, physically, from ancient Greeks and Romans.

Although we have some idea about European images of America and Native Americans through the artifacts they collected and artists' impressions, perhaps the allegorical representations of America, which began to appear in the 1570s, offer the best evidence about the impact of the "New World" on the European imagination. In these cases, artists emphasized the most representative features of America in such a way that their work reveals what objects and stereotypes were uppermost in the European mentality of the time.

Illustrations in the geographer and mapmaker Abraham Ortelius's *Theatrum Orbis Terrarum* (1570), the first printed atlas in European history, shockingly dramatized these opinions. America appears on the title page, portrayed as a recumbent woman with bow and arrows and a feathered hat, holding a severed head in her hand. At about the same time (1575), the French artist Etienne Delaune provided a more distinctive representation of America, presenting it as a woman dressed only in a feathered headdress, holding a bow, and her club and a crouching long-necked animal, presumably a llama, lay on the ground beside her. In 1581, two Flemish printmakers also represented America as a nude female. Philippe Galle depicted her as an Amazon with a human head dangling from her hand and a severed arm beneath her feet. Jan Sadeler engraved a drawing of a naked woman holding an arrow, seated beneath a tree where parrots perched, with a mountainous landscape behind with figures dredging gold dust in a river.

Other artists aimed at a composite image, combining as many characteristics of America as possible into one work—naked figures, cannibals, gold, and exotic plants and animals. Some artists even included the Aztec rite of human sacrifice, while others portrayed strange animals, including tapirs and sloths. The creation of a single composition to represent all of the various aspects of the American image proved to be a much more difficult task, however. The Dutch artist Maarten de Vos, for example, imagined America as a naked girl riding sidesaddle on a large armadillo. Another artist, the Italian Stefano della Bella, harnessed a pair of armadillos to a chariot driven by "America" on one of the playing cards he etched in 1644 to teach the young French king Louis XIV the foundations of geography and history. Some artists, however, apparently confused the armadillo with the rhinoceros, which appeared in several allegories of America. Similar confusion about the size of the tapir seems to be behind the choice of an elephant as the emblem of Brazil. Sometimes the figure of America is accompanied by an alligator.

Different kinds of Native Americans often appeared as single figures on maps, in illustrations and title pages to books about America, and even in French and Italian costume books which distinguished among styles of featherwork. "Typical" natives appeared, flanked by Columbus and Vespucci, in the clouds above an early-seventeenth-century vision of Cuba, with natives smoking tobacco in the foreground and others pushing barrows of gold ore across the beach. Among these Native Americans, a Canary Islander carries sugar cane on his shoulder, a Floridian holds a bow and arrow and a snake, a Patagonian swallows an arrow, a Chilean brandishes a club in his hand, a Brazilian gnaws a human foot next to bundles of brazilwood, a Peruvian grasps gold mining tools, and an Eskimo stands with his fishing spear and kayak. In the center sits America herself, dressed only in feathers, holding necklaces in one hand and a bow in the other. This, above all, was the image which established itself in the European imagination as "America."

Decorations for festivals frequently included allegories of America as well. When Francisco de Medici married Joanna of Austria in 1565, a triumphal arch set up in Florence included a painting of a partially clad nymph in the midst of some strange-looking animals, probably representing Peru. Three years later, for the christening of their son, Francisco and Joanna commissioned paintings of the conversion of New Spain (Mexico) to Christianity and an allegory of the River Plate to decorate the Florentine Baptistry. In 1598 the Florentine government observed the death of King Philip II of Spain with a solemn requiem in the church of San Lorenzo, which was decorated with representations of the continents, including a feathered America holding a rattle and a large painting depicting Philip II receiving ambassadors from America. When the famous Flemish painter Peter Paul Rubens decorated the city of Antwerp for the official entry of the new governor of the Netherlands in 1635, he designed an archway for the city mint in the form of the mountain of Potosí and its famous silver mines.

Court festivals sometimes made more specific allusions to America. For example, in 1613, lawyers associated with the Inns of Court in London, who had invested in the Virginia Company and wanted royal support for their enterprise, lobbied King James I with a play, *The Memorable Masque*. Set in Jamestown, it began with rocks drawn aside to reveal "Virginian Princes" dressed in silver cloth embroidered with suns, seated in a gold mine, and addressing a hymn to the setting sun, after which they turned to salute James. In 1685, American colonies formed the subject of the ballet, *The Temple of Peace*, presented to King Louis XIV of France at Fontainebleau. The natives of the French provinces in America who appeared in it represented not only Canadian natives but also the inhabitants of the vast area of Louisiana which La Salle had explored and claimed for France (naming it after the king) only three years earlier. At one point in the ballet, one of the natives stepped forward to address Louis in the following terms: "We have crossed the vast bosom of the ocean to render homage to the most powerful of kings . . . His name is revered by savage nations to the remotest shores. Everything echoes to the renown of his exploits. Ah! it is sweet to live under his laws."

Allegories of America served religious as well as political purposes in the late sixteenth century. In paintings of the continents done in 1595, for example, a half-naked Native American holding a crucifix in one hand and a bow in the other, while his companions roast human flesh, represented America. Not until the mid-seventeenth century, however, did the first truly memorable image linking Europeans' new worldview to Catholicism appear: Gian Lorenzo Bernini's famous fountain in the Piazza Navona in Rome. Gigantic figures seated around the rocky base of the fountain represent the four great rivers and continents: the Danube for Europe, the Nile for Africa, the Ganges for Asia, and the Plate for America. A characteristic animal accompanies each one. The River Plate wears a jeweled band on his right leg, gold coins tumble out of the rock on which he sits, a prickly pear sprouts by his foot, and an armadillo waddles out of a cavern below. He looks up at the obelisk, a symbol of divine light and eternity, crowned by a dove which signifies the Holy Ghost (and which also represented the personal emblem of Pope Innocent X). The central rock on which it stands is associated, however, with the hill of Calvary and the four rivers with those of Paradise. Thus, Bernini interwove the idea of salvation under the cross with the theme of Catholic triumph over the four parts of the world.

Sometimes the theme of evangelization carried over to secular paintings referring to America. A highly imaginative evocation of the landing of Columbus painted in the Duke of Genoa's palace depicts the raising of the cross, for example, before which Native Americans fall in admiration. Most painted allegories of

America and the other continents, however, remained secular and illustrated the expansion of human knowledge rather than the power of the church. The Flemish artist Jan van Kessel composed an outstanding series of such paintings in the mid-1660s. In particular, one devoted to America contains a treasure of geographical information (and misinformation). Its central panel represents an ideal collection of American curiosities, crammed with birds, fishes, beasts, reptiles, insects, shells, weapons, and armor. Many of the items are incorrectly classified, however, because the artist confused symbols of America with those of Asia, even at this late date. A woman and child dancing through a door, two statues in niches, and a depiction of suttee (the Indian practice in which a widow commits suicide by throwing herself on her husband's funeral pyre) are not American, but derived from a late sixteenth-century book of travels to the Portuguese East Indies.

The very existence of Native Americans, a people unknown to Europeans before the Age of Exploration, constituted a stunning new fact which had to be reconciled with traditional European assumptions about the origin and early history of all human life on earth. In the Renaissance, European scholars attempted to place Native Americans within a familiar context by relating them to various peoples of the world, including their own ancestors. At the time, the task simply overwhelmed even the most intelligent observers of the American scene, and as a result, their conclusions lack consistency. For Europeans, Native American society represented everything from a near-perfect civilization to the devil's playground. In all cases, however, Europeans evaluated Native American society according to their own standards, so their judgments primarily reflect their own definitions and standards of savagery and civilization, barbarism and humanity. Despite this self-centered and narrow vision, however, the European encounter with Native Americans inevitably sharpened Europeans' awareness of the great diversity of human customs and practices throughout the world and, as a result, forced them to reexamine their own values and beliefs.

4 / EUROPEAN DAILY LIFE AND AMERICA

> And as there are discovered new regions, new kingdoms, and new provinces by our Spaniards, they have brought unto us new medicines and new remedies wherewith they cure and make whole many infirmities, which if we lack them, were incurable, and without any remedy.
>
> NICOLÁS MONARDES
> *Joyfull Newes out of the Newe Founde Worlde* (1565)

While historians continue to debate the character and extent of America's impact on European economic, political, and intellectual developments, they have reached a consensus about the American influence on the more routine, yet very important, aspects of daily life. For millions of ordinary Europeans, the exploration and conquest of America meant a more varied and nutritious diet and new medicines, but also a new and terrifying disease. The ways in which Europeans responded to these positive and negative elements in their lives provide valuable insights about European attitudes towards America and help define more precisely the nature of the American impact on all levels of European society.

AMERICAN FOODS AND EUROPEAN LIFE

Almost immediately after finding an island in the Bahamas in 1492, Christopher Columbus began to study and describe the plants and foods of America. In his log, he reported how he walked among trees that were the most beautiful he had ever seen, although they were as different from those he knew in Europe as day from night. He thought the same thing about the fruits, the herbs, and even the rocks of this unfamiliar world.

By 19 October, he declared that he simply did not know where to go next, and that he never tired of looking at such luxurious vegetation, "which is so different from ours." With considerable foresight, Columbus guessed that he had found many plants and trees that could be worth a lot in Spain for use as dyes, spices, and medicines, but he also admitted that he could not recognize them. As a result of his ignorance, he decided to try to bring back a sample of everything he could.

During his stay in the Bahamas, Columbus ate an iguana (he said the meat was white and tasted like chicken), sweet potatoes (which he compared to carrots and said they tasted like chestnuts), maize (which he compared to millet), manioc, in the form of cassava bread (which he thought was made from yams), and chili peppers. Columbus had trouble distinguishing among the various roots and tubers of tropical America, but he began a process that eventually changed the dietary habits of literally millions of Europeans.

The basic diet of Europeans before 1492 had remained rather constant for a very long time. Indeed, it had been established in the period following the Neolithic era (approximately 20,000 B.C. to 10,000 B.C.) and consisted primarily of wheat, barley, oats, and rye. In the wake of Columbus's voyages all of this changed. The European diet became rich and varied. Just consider this list of products that originated in America and found their way, eventually, into Europeans' lives: maize (corn), various kinds of beans (especially "French" beans and lima beans), peanuts, potatoes, sweet potatoes, manioc (cassava and tapioca), squashes, pumpkins, papaya, guava, avocado, pineapple, tomatoes, red and green chile peppers, chocolate, turkey, vanilla, and, unfortunately, tobacco. Most of these items came from Central and South America. In the early sixteenth century, North America also provided a great abundance and new varieties of fish (as well as animal furs and timber). Collectively, these products made the single most valuable addition to Europe's ability to produce food since the very beginnings of agriculture. As far as dietary habits are concerned, no other series of events in all world history brought as much significant change as did European overseas expansion.

On his first voyage, Columbus did not record a great deal of botanical information. He apparently noticed only those familiar plants which he could associate with European species, such as palm trees and groves of pines. The case is different on his second voyage, however. Here his botanical observations became much sharper and more accurate, probably because of the influence of an Italian companion, Guglielmo Coma. Among other things, Coma became interested in maize (he published the first description of it in Europe in 1494); and upon leaving the West Indies, he took seeds of the plant back to Europe. As a result, Spaniards and other Europeans soon began cultivating the plant. In 1530 the Spanish historian Gonzalo Fernández de Oviedo saw it growing on an estate in Madrid. Indeed, it became so well established early in the sixteenth century that several botanists simply assumed that it came from Asia rather than America—it is still called *granoturco* (Turkish grain) in Italy. Because of its large yield per acre, farmers grew it primarily as feed for livestock. Maize entered the human diet only in parts of Italy and Romania; in other areas it eventually transformed agriculture and indeed the whole economy of the country as an animal feed.

Of all American plants imported into Europe in the sixteenth century, the potato had one of the most interesting histories. It began as a rare and exotic luxury and eventually became the staple diet of the poor. In 1493 Columbus brought back sweet potatoes from Hispaniola. They adapted successfully to Spain, which imported greater quantities in subsequent years. Sweet potatoes became much prized for both their taste and supposed aphrodisiac effects. This plant (*Ipomoea batatas*), however, is botanically distinct from the common potato (*Solanum tuberosum*), which no European seems to have encountered until 1536 when Gonzalo Jiménez de Quesada led an expedition to the interior of Colombia and captured the city of Bogotá, capital of the Chibcha kingdom. He found that the inhabitants of this high plateau lived on maize, beans, and what one of the invading party (Juan de Castellanos) called truffles. Truffles are floury roots of good flavor produced by plants with scanty flowers of a dull purple color. Two years later, Pedro Cieza de León found potatoes near Popayán and published a description of the potato for the first time. He said its roots were almost like truffles and, when cooked, had a soft pulp like a roasted chestnut.

Spanish conquistadors soon recognized the virtues of the potato, either in its fresh or *chuñu* form.[1] Slaves in the silver mines of Potosí (in modern-day Bolivia) subsisted almost entirely on *chuñu*, and before long speculators streamed across the Atlantic from Spain to buy supplies of potatoes from the growers in the mountains. The speculators resold them at inflated prices to the mine workers and then returned home considerably richer for their trouble. As soon as the Spanish government began to organize its shipping to carry away the wealth of the Peruvian mines, it adopted potatoes as basic ships' stores: the return journey sometimes took up to four months. Returning ships, therefore, carried the plant to Europe and cultivated it there very soon after the conquest of Peru. No one knows exactly when cultivation and consumption began in Europe, but by 1573 the Hospital de la Sangre at Seville, where Spanish trade with America was concentrated, began feeding potatoes to its patients, and potatoes may have been grown and consumed in Spain even before this time.

From Spain, the potato quickly spread to other countries, and by the early 1580s it had ceased to be an exotic luxury item. It found its way to Italy, where it became used as a garden vegetable by 1588. By 1601, according to the botanist Jules Charles de l'Ecluse, people did not even treat potatoes as a delicacy but cooked them with mutton in the same manner as they did turnips and carrots. It is known that the potato reached England by 1586, when Sir Walter Raleigh reportedly sent them from America to his Irish estate at Youghal for cultivation and experimentation; but in light of close commercial ties between Spain and Ireland,

---

1 *Chuñu* was a way of preserving potatoes developed by native Andean peoples which combined an alternating freezing and drying process. When the crop had been harvested, the potatoes were spread out on the ground and left overnight in the biting open air. The next day, great numbers of men, women, and children assembled to tread out the moisture from them. The same process was repeated for the next four or five days, after which the potatoes, now freed from much of their water content, were finally dried and stored.

potatoes quite possibly had reached Ireland from Spain at an earlier date.

In the early seventeenth century, the potato became even more popular in some European circles. Doctor Tobias Venner said that the nourishment it yielded, although somewhat "windy," was very substantial, good and "restorative"; and William Salmon claimed that it stopped fluxes of the bowels, was full of nutrients, and cured consumption (tuberculosis). On the other hand, in 1619 the French government of Burgundy banned potatoes because people believed that too frequent use of them caused leprosy. This idea persisted in France until well into the eighteenth century, and people of other regions attributed various ills to the vegetable. The Swiss, who ate large quantities of potatoes, blamed them for scrofula (a form of tuberculosis that afflicts the lymphatic glands rather than the lungs). In general, not until the mid-eighteenth century, when grain prices increased and a growing population strained the food supply, did Europeans fully appreciate the potato's nutritional value. Particularly in Scotland and Ireland, its use became more general—with disastrous results when the crop failed because of disease in 1845. That a potato famine should have driven thousands of Irish families to emigrate to America is one of the great ironies of history.

Perhaps no American food is a better illustration of some of the strange notions that Europeans had about American foods than the tomato. The first written mention of the tomato appeared in a commentary on the ancient Greek botanist Dioscorides by Petrus Matthiolus in 1544. He considered the tomato a species of mandrake recently brought to Italy and prepared like eggplant: fried in oil with salt and pepper. Matthiolus apparently got his information secondhand, but others frequently repeated his "recipe."

By the 1570s, tomatoes had acquired an excellent reputation for medicinal properties. The Italian Melchior Guilandini declared that they were useful as treatments for rheumatism and similar ailments, and German medical authorities agreed. In 1588, for example, Joachim Camerarius said that it was effective against scabies (a highly contagious skin disease). For his part, J. T. Tabernaemontanus thought that tomato juice was an effective remedy for St. Anthony's fire and other "fluxes." Other experts, no doubt influenced by the plant's erroneous Latin name (*pomum amoris*), concluded that it must be an aphrodisiac, or at least so beautiful as to "command love." How else could it have acquired the name love apple?

Sixteenth-century Europeans had little interest in the food value of tomatoes. Generally, they considered them nothing more than a curiosity with some ornamental value. In 1666, however, Dominicus Chabraeus wrote a book in which he listed the tomato under malignant and poisonous plants; its foliage belongs to the deadly nightshade family and does contain dangerous alkaloids. This reputation lasted until the late eighteenth century, when the great Swedish scientist Linnaeus called attention to the fact that people were known to eat tomatoes without suffering any ill effects. Nevertheless, most authorities on botany continued to harbor suspicions about the wisdom of eating tomatoes.

While these experts were debating the value of tomatoes, ordinary gardeners grew them in ever-increasing numbers and enjoyed the fruits of their labors. Eventually the tomato's reputation improved. In 1819, Joseph Sabine reported to the Royal Horticultural Society in England that great use had been made of tomatoes for culinary purposes and that the plants were being grown in private and commercial gardens. He thought that the tomato possessed an "agreeable acid" appropriate for use in soups and salads as well as "in the manner of ketchup." According to Henry Philips in 1820, a certain John Wilmot had harvested 433 bushels of tomatoes the previous year, and some of them measured twelve inches in circumference. By 1836, chops with tomato sauce was a dish of sufficient popularity to be mentioned in Charles Dickens's *Pickwick Papers*.

Ironically, the fruit that found its way to Europe from America was not seen on the dinner tables of eighteenth- and early-nineteenth-century American colonists. Most feared it for much the same reasons that Chabraeus wrote about in the seventeenth century. Yet, if any one man liberated the tomato in America and enabled us to enjoy it in the dishes that Europeans had been eating since the time they first brought it home from their sea voyages, it was Colonel Robert Gibbon Johnson of Salem, New

Jersey. Johnson brought the tomato plant to New Jersey farmers after a trip abroad in 1808. But he saw that most regarded it as an ornamental bush and continued to avoid the the fruit as part of their diet. Johnson persisted, and in 1830 he proposed to appear on the Salem courthouse steps and eat not one, but an entire basket of "wolf peaches," as he called them.

Public reaction to Johnson's antics was immediate. His physician declared that the "foolish colonel will foam and froth at the mouth and double over with appendicitis. All that oxalic acid! One dose and you're dead." Nonetheless, Johnson ate the entire basket of wolf peaches, and his efforts turned the tide for the tomato, which began appearing regularly in U.S. markets by 1835. But prejudices lingered, and still do. As late as 1860, the popular *Godey's Lady's Book* warned readers that tomatoes "should be cooked for 3 hours" before eating, and the myth still persists that tomatoes make the blood acid.

One of the first judgments that Europeans made about Native Americans was that they ate disgusting foods, including "large, fat spiders," and worms that breed in rotten wood and other decayed objects. In fact, Native Americans living in tropical America had a long tradition of eating the insects that abounded in those areas. Indeed, the Aztecs considered the agave worm a delicacy. When Columbus encountered the Taino natives in the Caribbean, he also discovered zamia bread—most probably one of the "other decayed objects."

Native Americans made zamia bread by grating the stems of the zamia plant and then shaping the pulp into balls that they left in the sun for two or three days until the balls began to rot, turn black, and become wormy. After the balls of pulp ripened, Native Americans flattened them out and baked them on a griddle over a fire. The Tainos believed that if the bread were eaten before it turned black and became infested with worms, the eaters would die. They knew what they were talking about: unless zamia pulp is fermented or very thoroughly washed, it can be highly toxic.

Bread made in Cuba from an equally poisonous plant, the bitter variety of manioc, pleased the Spaniards more. The natives peeled and grated the roots of this plant and squeezed out the unhealthy juices. Then they boiled the roots to make cassareep sauce and also threw in a sediment to make tapioca. In addition, they strained the pulp and shaped it into flat cakes, which they cooked slowly on a griddle. The resulting soft and flexible bread, cassava, could then be dried and kept for two or three years. The Spaniards, and later the French, adopted cassava enthusiastically, and some Europeans even claimed that it was better than bread made from wheat.

Perhaps the American fruit which aroused the most interest in Europe was the pineapple. A consignment arrived in Spain early in the sixteenth century, and Peter Martyr reported that King Ferdinand found it superior in taste to all other fruit. The plant could easily be grown in Spain or Italy; but in England, artists commemorated the presentation of an imported specimen to the king almost as if it were some outsized, precious jewel.

In Mexico, Hernándo Cortés and his troops encountered an Aztec drink called "chocolatl" made from cocoa beans. According to European reports, Montezuma's household went through two thousand jars of cocoa bean paste a day. It quickly spread to Spain in the form that the Aztecs used—as a beverage. In Mexico, the Aztecs had made little cakes of this paste and mixed them with water in a gourd until they foamed. Apparently enamored of the food, they gulped down the unsweetened drink in one swallow. Spanish eyewitnesses said that the drink gave the natives strength and vigor, and that those who were used to drinking it could not remain robust without it even if they ate other substantial things. Moreover, their strength seemed to diminish when they did not drink their chocolate. Rich in fat, the cocoa bean was a good food source for the Aztecs.

In seventeenth-century Spain, the preparation of a cup of chocolate became a complex procedure. Instructions written in 1631 required that every hundred cocoa beans had to be mixed with two pods of chili or Mexican pepper, or two peppercorns, a handful of aniseed, some cinnamon, a dozen almonds and a dozen hazelnuts, half a pound of sugar, and powder made from several varieties of flowers (the combination of cocoa bean and sugar itself is symbolic of the intermingling of New World and Old World). Spain exported the drink to Italy and Flanders, but not until 1659 did chocolate become widely known in France. At first the French court greeted it enthusiastically—

encouraged by the fact that the University of Paris medical faculty had given it a stamp of approval. Chocolate remained a beverage in Europe for almost three hundred years after its introduction to Europe. Not until the 1820s did Dutchman Conrad von Houten press the oil from the cocoa beans, thus creating cocoa powder, which lead to a form of chocolate that readily absorbed sugar. In the 1840s, an English firm created "eating chocolate," which became popular with the masses.

As it had been for centuries, fish continued to be the most important of all articles of trade in the fifteenth and sixteenth centuries. Monasteries and members of the upper class had their own fish ponds; but for most people, dried or salted fish constituted a vital food in the winter and on certain religious holidays throughout the year. Because ocean fishing was a major industry, the gradual failure of the Baltic herring fishery set European fishermen, from all parts of the continent, searching the coastal waters of Europe and Iceland, and venturing far out into the Atlantic. Certainly by the late fifteenth century, Europeans had found their way to the great cod-fishing banks off the coast of Newfoundland. Fishing fleets from England, France, Portugal, and Holland frequented the area from then on, using the island as a base and place to dry the catch for transport back to Europe.

Fish represented cheap animal protein, and dried cod provided the cheapest fish in most places. Cod could easily be flaked and cured; after being cured, it would keep and ship well, even in the tropics or the Mediterranean in summertime. Of all the resources of America, cod from the Newfoundland fishing Banks, the coast of Labrador, and the Gulf of St. Lawrence proved the most immediately exploitable and also the most beneficial to Europe for centuries. At the end of the fifteenth century, both John Cabot (in 1497) and Gaspar Corte Real (in 1500) reported that Newfoundland waters literally teemed with codfish. For example, Cabot reported that all he had to do was lower a weighted basket into the water and lift it out. On 18 June 1534, one of Jacques Cartier's ships caught more than a hundred big codfish on the west coast of Newfoundland in less than an hour.

As the number of ships on the Banks increased, the nature of the trade changed from the immediate sale of "green" fish to the marketing, at longer intervals, of much larger quantities of "dry" fish. Fishermen set up temporary shelters ashore during the summer months in order to dry and repair nets and smoke and salt the catch. They paid no attention to the territorial claims of Portugal, which had built no forts and conducted no naval patrols in the area. The beaches of the Newfoundland coast became the regular seasonal campsites of a tough and independent cosmopolitan fishing community.

The development of the North Atlantic fisheries had effects of far-reaching significance, both within Europe and in the story of European expansion. Obviously, the influx of great quantities of cod in itself constituted a significant economic event, especially in a continent where many people lived near the starvation level for part of every year. Although cod had been known in Europe before the sixteenth century, catches off Newfoundland and the coast of New England became so large, and dried and salted codfish so well preserved, that fish could be marketed at very low prices. It became a regular diet of the poor, and to some extent, it took the place of herring on days of abstinence.

The seasonal fishing-camps also became centers for barter with the natives, and the trade in furs grew up as a profitable sideline of the fishery. A natural desire to increase the effective length of the fishing and fur-trading season gave rise to plans, like those of Sir Humphrey Gilbert in the later sixteenth century, to replace the seasonal camps with permanent settlements in Newfoundland and other parts of North America. As a rule, however, these plans did not come from the fishing community; skippers of fishing craft were not long-term planners. They organized their business around making a full catch during the summer months and getting back home with it before the fall storms. Therefore, they most bitterly opposed any scheme for putting colonies in North America because settlers might compete with seasonal fishermen by fishing for a greater part of the year.

The increase in the number of ships and men fitted for long and hazardous ocean passages amounted to the most important result of recourse to the Banks. In Tudor England, for example, a whole series of government regulations referred to the fisheries as a nursery of ships and seamen. Sailors who gained their experience in fishing off the Banks manned the ships that sought the northern passage and opened trade with Russia, the expeditions which began the settlement of North America, and the English and Dutch fleets which defeated the navies of Spain.

Sugar also became one of the most sought-after products from America with far-reaching significance. A cheaper sweetening agent than honey, sugar helped popularize the drinking of coffee, tea, and chocolate in Europe. It also revolutionized cooking. Around 1492, for example, European apothecaries generally sold sugar because its scarcity made it so expensive that only the rich could afford it. By order of King Ferdinand, Columbus introduced sugar to the New World when he took sugar cane from Spain's Canary Islands to Hispaniola on his second voyage, and more plants arrived early in the sixteenth century. The Spanish historian Oviedo reported that the first sugar mill on Hispaniola, a small one using horses for power, was built about 1509, and that the owner brought sugar workers from the Canary Islands. Hispaniola seemed to have been the perfect spot for cultivating sugar. It had an ideal climate, fertile soil, and abundant supplies of water and firewood. As a result, the first mill prospered, and others followed in rapid succession. By 1547 twenty large mills operated in Hispaniola, presumably powered by water, and four smaller mills used horses. By the middle of the sixteenth century, Cuba, Jamaica, Mexico, and Brazil produced sugar, and Spanish ships carried such large amounts of sugar home that Spain became self-sufficient in the product. No other plant from the eastern side of the Pacific Ocean found such a favorable environment in America as sugar cane.

Sugar became interdependent with the slave trade very soon after 1492. As early as 1506, Spain had begun cultivating sugar in the greater Antilles—especially in Cuba and Hispaniola. As the Native American population in these regions died off in great numbers, the Spaniards (who preferred to avoid manual labor themselves) imported slaves from Africa as replacement labor. After a short time, however, as the Spaniards became more interested in gold and silver than in sugar, the Portuguese took full advantage of the potential profitability of sugar production in America. As a result, the Portuguese have the dubious honor of truly combining sugar production with the African slave trade.

Indeed, the Portuguese had been able to monopolize the slave trade with a clear conscience. As early as the mid-fifteenth century, Pope Nicholas V had authorized them to attack, conquer, and enslave the Moslims, pagans, and other enemies of Christ who lived in Africa south of Cape Bojador, including the entire coast of Guinea. The native political and economic elite on the Gold Coast of Africa also proved only too eager to exchange slaves for European cloth, hardware, alcohol, and weapons. By 1526, however, even Mbemba Nzinga, the ruler of the Congo and an enthusiastic convert to Christianity, protested to the Portuguese that local merchants were kidnapping his own people to exchange for European products, and he asked the Portuguese government to stop the trade. His request went unheeded because the Portuguese required ever-increasing amounts of slave labor to cultivate sugar. In 1550, Portuguese colonies in Brazil had 5 sugar plantations; in 1623, the number had increased to 350.

In the seventeenth century, European interest in both sugar production and the slave trade increased. In 1635 the Dutch invaded and occupied the northern part of Brazil and a few years later took the Gold Coast from Portugal. Although they lost their foothold in Brazil in 1654, they had learned a great deal about sugar production. The English, French, and Danes took possession of several Caribbean islands, and soon they also learned, from the Dutch, how to profit from the production of sugar.

The demand for African slaves to work the new plantations increased dramatically. For example, historians have estimated that before 1600 fewer than 1 million African slaves had been imported to the Americas. In the seventeenth century, the number increased to about 2.75 million; and in the eighteenth century, the slave population reached about 7 million. By this time, of course, planters used slaves not only to cultivate sugar but also tobacco and cotton on the mainland of North America.

European competition over sugar brought to an end that phase of imperialism which had begun with competition over spices. At the beginning, sugar had been unimportant—a minor luxury for Europeans. The development of plantations in America, however, came just when supplies of Europe's traditional sweetener, honey, were dwindling, partly as a result of the

Protestant Reformation's hostility to monasteries, whose need for beeswax candles had placed them among Europe's most important producers of honey. As soon as the availability of sugar grew, so did its popularity. Indeed, its popularity increased even more when Europeans learned that it could be used to preserve fruit (around 1600) and to make jam (sometime before 1730). Sugar became so important to trade that in the 1670s the Dutch yielded New Amsterdam (the future New York City) to England in exchange for sugar-producing Surinam, and in 1763 France was prepared to cede all of Canada to England in exchange for sugar-producing Guadeloupe.

AMERICAN PLANTS AND EUROPEAN LIFE

As a result of the European exploration and conquest of America, many plants of a purely decorative kind began to appear in Europe, and they acclimatized so easily in gardens that their origin was easily forgotten. For example, Nicolás Monardes wrote of the novelty of the common sunflower from Florida in 1565; but by about 1633, the artist Anthony Van Dyck used it quite naturally and informally in his self-portrait to represent the royal patronage of the English king Charles I beaming down on him. Its relative, first seen on Cape Cod by the French explorer Samuel de Champlain in 1605 and introduced into France between 1609 and 1617, reached England under the double disguise of a "Jerusalem artichoke."

Indeed, America continued to be Europe's main source of exotic plants until the nineteenth century when botanists first explored Central Asia, China, and Japan. Moreover, coming from high altitudes in the tropics and the temperate zone, American exotics could easily be acclimated in Europe, unlike plants from Africa and India. Dogwood and the first of the passion flowers arrived before the end of the seventeenth century; magnolias, with their glossy leaves and huge lemon-scented blossoms, in the early eighteenth century; and ornate dahlias with quilled petals, which had been hybridized in Aztec gardens, arrived in the 1790s. Such a steady supply of outstanding horticultural novelties could hardly fail to keep alive the image of America as a land of unequaled natural riches.

Since few European students of natural history could travel to America, most studied imported specimens and relied on the reports of travelers, few of whom had much scientific knowledge. For example, Monardes, who was the Spanish physician who popularized the medicinal uses of tobacco, could only describe those American plants which he saw growing in his garden in Seville. Based on this evidence, he nevertheless extolled the therapeutic virtues of a long list of American plants, some known in Europe only as dried bark, leaves, or gums: sarsaparilla, sassafras, cocoa, copal and other aromatic balsams, and guaiacum. Some seventy years later Jacques Philippe Cornut based his pioneering work on the flora of Canada on what he could see in the gardens of Paris. Clearly, scientists needed a properly equipped scientific exploration to America. King Philip II of Spain, therefore, dispatched an expedition to America under the leadership of the physician and naturalist Francisco Hernández in 1571. Hernández spent seven years in America making a comprehensive survey of medicinal plants throughout Spanish America, including their identities, uses, cultivation, and distribution. He then returned to Seville with a written description of some twelve thousand plants—with illustrations. (Unfortunately, the findings of his expedition remained unpublished until 1649.) Meanwhile the French botanist l'Ecluse traveled to Spain, Portugal, England, and Austria in search of the new exotic American drugs, some of which he brought back to Amsterdam. He even persuaded owners of ships which returned with drugs from America to include in their crews in the future physicians, surgeons, and expert druggists who could accurately describe the habitat of plants and test their efficacy.

Among these scientific expeditions to America, the one organized by Count Johan Maurits of Nassau-Siegen, a Dutch administrator in Brazil in the mid-seventeenth century, is of prime importance. He sent a team of scientists and artists to study and record all aspects of the natural history of Brazil, and with this expedition the interests of scientists and the efforts of artists came together. The best known of the artists employed by Count Maurits, Frans Post, made numerous drawings of the Brazilian landscape on the spot, then continued painting it from his notes and memory long after he returned to Holland. The scientists in the group included the botanist William Pies (better known as Piso), and Georg Marcgrave, an astronomer and artist who painted numerous careful watercolors of flora and fauna. The results of their combined researches, published in Leiden in 1648 at the expense of Count Maurits, provided the first full and accurate account of the natural history of any part of America—and one that remained a standard work for a century and a half.

Inspired by the Aztec's gardens in Tenochtitlan (modern Mexico City), European zoologists and botanists tried to establish their own collections of flora and fauna. In his published letters, Cortés described with wonder Montezuma's numerous ponds in which every type of waterfowl was kept, the large cages for birds of prey and animals, the gardens of herbs and flowers, and the six hundred men employed to attend them. Renaissance Europe contained gardens and menageries, of course, but none on such a grand scale. Not surprisingly, the first botanical garden in Europe appeared in 1545 in Padua—the university city near Venice—where scholars took a keen interest in new geographical and botanical information. Naturalists such as the Italian Ulisse Aldrovandi, who had a special interest in America, recognized the need to study and categorize these new flora and fauna. Aldrovandi founded a botanical garden in Bologna in 1568 and established the first European museum of natural history in his own house. Indeed, he planned a scientific expedition to America with the support, he hoped, of the Grand Duke of Tuscany (who, in addition to owning a collection of Mexican works of art, also boasted American flora and fauna in his gardens and menagerie). The classification of this fascinating flora did not lead to any radical changes in European scientific theory, but findings in America may have accelerated somewhat the decline of respect for the botanical authorities from ancient Greece and Rome, who, of course, knew nothing about America.

While some American plants could easily be associated with European counterparts, tobacco constituted a complete novelty. When Columbus arrived in Cuba in November 1492 he saw the natives smoking rolled tobacco leaves, and he remarked on the practice. Most of the European travelers who followed him to America also described the strange practice of "drinking smoke." Perhaps the Italian Girolamo Benzoni, who visited America in the second half of the sixteenth century, provides the most vivid of these accounts:

> The smoke goes into the mouth, the throat, the head, and they retain it as long as they can, for they find a pleasure in it, and so much do they fill themselves with this cruel smoke, that they lose their reason. And there are some that take so much of it that they fall down as if they were dead, and remain the greater part of the day or night stupefied. Some men are found who are content with imbibing only enough of this smoke to make them giddy, and no more. See what a pestiferous and wicked poison from the devil this must be.[2]

By the time that Benzoni's description appeared in print (in the 1570s) the tobacco habit had caught on throughout Europe. For a fairly long time, however, it remained an object of curiosity in botanical gardens. As early as 1554, the German scientist Konrad Gesner was raising tobacco plants from seeds, and he even had a watercolor drawing made of one of them. In 1560, the French ambassador to Lisbon, Jean Nicot (whose name gives us the word nicotine), sent tobacco powder to Catherine de Medici to use for relief of migraine headaches, according to Portuguese practice. Another Frenchman, André Thevet, who brought the plant to France, asserted that the natives of Brazil used it to eliminate superfluous fluids from the brain.

In 1565, Nicolás Monardes, the Spanish naturalist and physician who had gained first-hand experience with American plants at Seville, published a book on their therapeutic value. His *Joyfull Newes out of the Newe Founde Worlde* not only took the medical world by storm but influenced medical thought and practice for nearly a century. Although only the first chapter of the book dealt with tobacco (the second chapter covered sassafras, to which he also attributed incredible healing powers), it became famous for its treatment of that subject. Drawing on native lore, tales told by returning colonists, and his own fertile imagination, Monardes claimed that tobacco had cured or could cure headaches (including migraine headaches),

---

2 Girolamo Benzoni, *History of the New World*, trans. and ed. W. H. Smyth (London: The Hakluyt Society, 1857), 81.

rheumatism, pains in any part of the body, stomachache, asthma, shortness of breath, obstructions in the chest or intestines, gas pains, colic in children or adults, poisonous bites and stings, abscesses, carbuncles, tumors, fresh wounds, old sores, burns, chilblains, ringworm of the scalp, and dropsy. According to Monardes, tobacco would also kill or expel worms, stop bleeding, and counteract poisons—even those deadly ones used by the Caribs on their arrowheads that were destined to baffle medical science for generations. By slowly chewing little balls of tobacco, he said, natives could walk for three or four days through desolate country without liquids or food and not suffer from thirst or hunger; and pellets of tobacco inserted in dental cavities would kill the pain and stop decay. Medical tracts written in the last quarter of the sixteenth century and in 1601 to 1602 repeated and enlarged Monardes's claims for tobacco by adding gout and syphilis to the ills that it could cure, and even claimed that it would keep a man awake and put him to sleep, sharpen his appetite and suppress his hunger.

In England, the great Elizabethan author Edmund Spenser referred to "divine tobacco," and Thomas Hariot reported that it purged "superfluous phlegm and other gross humours" and that it opened all the pores and passages of the body. Perhaps impressed by this publicity, Thomas Hariot became a heavy smoker—frequent purchases of tobacco appear in his papers (he died of cancer of the mouth). Not surprisingly, the habit of smoking spread rapidly among members of the upper class, popularized by Sir Walter Raleigh and those in touch with the American colonies. Indeed, Raleigh's last act was to take a pipeful of tobacco before he went to the scaffold. Even before the end of Elizabeth's reign, the habit of smoking tobacco had spread to the lower levels of society. One eyewitness reported that at such lower-class amusements as bull-baiting, bear-whipping, and everywhere else the English are constantly smoking the "Nicotian weed," which in America is called tobacco. All of this, of course, was good for the English settlement in Virginia; tobacco sales put the colony on its feet and allowed it to survive. Perhaps the prevailing opinion about tobacco is best summed up in the following popular song:

Tobacco, tobacco, sing sweetly for tobacco!
Tobacco is like love, oh love it;
For you see, I will prove it.
Love maketh lean the fat man's tumour.
So doth tobacco.
Love still dries up the wanton humour,
So doth tobacco.
Love maketh men sail from shore to shore,
So doth tobacco.
'Tis fond love often makes men poor,
So doth tobacco.
Love makes men scorn all coward fears.
So doth tobacco.
Love often sets men by the ears,
So doth tobacco.
Tobacco, tobacco,
Sing sweetly for tobacco.
Tobacco is like love, oh love it;
For you see I have proved it.[3]

Given this kind of publicity, it is no wonder that tobacco spread rapidly throughout Europe. Brought into Spain around 1558 as a soothing drug, tobacco spread rapidly to France, England, Italy, the Balkans, and Russia. By the seventeenth century it had established itself as an essential medicinal product. Nevertheless, all kinds of prejudices and superstitions followed tobacco wherever it was introduced. Some thought it to be the most disgusting plant imported from the New World, and many termed the struggle against its popularity "the tobacco war." The obviously exaggerated claims on behalf of tobacco prompted King James I of England to write *A Counterblaste to Tobacco* in 1604. Here he denounced tobacco as harmful to the brain and dangerous to the lungs. James, one of the most active enemies of the new plant, also thought that tobacco turned the internal parts of the body into a "kitchen" and infested them with an oily and sticky soot.

AMERICAN ANIMALS AND EUROPEAN LIFE

Europeans found themselves fascinated by American animal life. Moreover, their descriptions of the various animals they encoun-

---

3 From Tobias Hume's *Musical Humours* (1605), cited in *The Renaissance Reader*, ed. J. B. Ross and M. M. McLaughlin (New York: Penguin Books, 1977), 161–62.

tered are important because they illuminate the Europeans' basic assumptions about nature in America. For example, for six-teenth-century mapmakers, images of brightly colored parrots and toucans represented the brilliance and beauty of America, while four-footed animals more frequently represented its exotic character. European perceptions of the llama provides a per-fect example of this process because it tested the descriptive powers of European authors. One of the earliest accounts of this animal comes from Antonio Pigafetta, who accompanied Magellan on his circumnavigation of the world (1519–22) and wrote an account of his experiences in 1525. Like so many things in America, Pigafetta found the animal to be rather strange, and he could only convey that impression to his readers by comparing the various parts of its body to those of other animals familiar to Europeans. Thus, according to Pigafetta, it had the head and ears of a mule, the neck and body of a camel, the legs of a deer, and the tail of a horse. Some strange beasts answering to this description appeared in the "Land of Peru" on a map drawn by Alonso de Santa Cruz in 1540. By 1551, the three types of llama—pacos (which yield alpaca wool), silky haired vicuñas, and gua-nacos, which also served as beasts of burden—seem to have been distinguished from one another on a world map by Sancho Gutiérrez. Europeans soon appreciated the value of these ani-mals, and they imported llamas to Europe. One is recorded in Antwerp as early as 1558. In 1562, the Italian sculptor Gianpolo Poggini, in Madrid, portrayed another llama as the emblem of Peru on the reverse of a medal of the Spanish king Philip II. Poggini wrote to a friend in Italy that he included it because it was such a rare and useful animal, giving wool, milk and meat, and bearing loads like a donkey.

Perhaps no single American animal exemplifies the confu-sion of Europeans in their attempts to distinguish things Ameri-can from Asian than the turkey. Columbus, who thought that he had reached the outlying regions of Asia, encountered—and tasted—turkeys in Central America in 1502. Within a quarter of a century, Europeans became familiar with this American bird. Peter Martyr, the first important historian of European expansion overseas, saw turkeys in Spain, and described how the males preened themselves before the females, like peacocks. By 1525, turkey merchants who traded in the eastern Mediterranean had brought turkeys to England, and in 1542 the great French writer François Rabelais described them as rich food, fit for royalty. Moreover, early sixteenth-century mapmakers sometimes used the image of the turkey to designate the typical animal life of North America on their maps.

Despite these indications of its American origin, however, many educated Europeans believed that the turkey originated in Asia rather than America. Indeed, two of Renaissance Europe's most respected ornithologists, the Swiss Konrad Gesner and the Frenchman Pierre Belon, regarded the turkey as an exotic Asian bird. Even the English turkey merchants, who may have been ignorant of the Mexican name for this creature—*uexolotl* (or perhaps merely reluctant to try to pronounce it)—simply called it the turkie-bird. Continental Europeans were no more clear on the subject. The French called the animal *coq d'Inde* (Indian cock), which they corrupted to *dinde* or *dindon*; while Italians and Germans used basically the same name (*galle d'India* and *indianische Henn*, respectively). Obviously, India had played no part in the transmission of the turkey from Mexico to Europe, but the fact that Europeans gave this American animal a name that associated it with Asia provides an excellent illustration of the difficulty Europeans had ridding themselves of old geographical misconceptions.

AMERICAN DISEASES AND EUROPEAN DAILY LIFE: THE CASE OF SYPHILIS

Questions of how and why syphilis suddenly appeared in Europe at the end of the fifteenth century are among the most controversial problems in the history of medicine. In general, there are two competing theories about its origins. Some scholars contend that Columbus brought syphilis back to Europe from America in 1493, but others believe that the strain of venereal syphilis which struck Renaissance Europe had existed there long before the voyages of exploration. Neither of these interpretations has completely conquered its rival, however, so the debate continues even today. For sixteenth-century Europeans, on the other hand, these issues did not appear to be nearly so difficult to solve. From the 1490s, they believed that a new disease had swept across Europe, and they named it according to the supposed place of origin. For example, the French called it the Neapolitan disease; the Italians and Germans called it the French disease; and the English called it the French or the Spanish disease. Everybody blamed the appearance of the disease on an alien group—they just could not agree on which one.

Among these terms for syphilis, "Spanish disease" is the most fascinating because it indicates what Europeans came to believe about the ultimate origin of the affliction. In 1518, a quarter of a century after the fact, a book published in Venice first mentioned the theory that a "Spanish disease" had been imported from America (or the West Indies) by sailors who accompanied Columbus on his first voyage in 1492–93. Indeed, two of the most important historians of the early Spanish empire in America, Bartolomé de las Casas and Gonzalo Fernández de Oviedo, both asserted that members of Columbus's crew had brought syphilis to Europe from America. Oviedo, himself, made several voyages to the West Indies and reported that he had found evidence of the new disease among Native Americans, and Las Casas claimed that the natives had told him that they had known the disease before the arrival of the Europeans. Both historians noted that the sickness appeared to be much less dangerous for the infected natives than for the Spaniards, a contrast one might expect if one group had long contact and exposure to it and the other none at all. Moreover, in 1539 the physician Rodrigo Diaz de Isla published a description of the "West Indian disease," and claimed to have treated at least one of Columbus's crew for it at Barcelona. In addition, Europeans observed that the most effective cure for the disease contained "holy wood" (guaiacum), a resin obtained from two evergreen trees (*Guaiacum officinale* and *Guaiacum sanctum*) that are native to South America and the West Indies. As a result, they concluded that the sickness must have originated in the same place where the remedy had been found.

The Italian Girolamo Fracastoro wrote the most important early work on syphilis in 1546. Even earlier, in the 1520s, he had published a long poem called *Fracastor, Syphilis or the French Disease*, thus giving the disease its modern name, derived from the imaginary shepherd Syphilis (although the term did not come into widespread use until the eighteenth century). In his important book, *On Contagion and Contagious Diseases* (1546), Fracastoro examined many contagious diseases, including syphilis. He described it as beginning with small ulcers on the genital organs, followed by a pustular rash, usually starting on the scalp. The pustules (small elevations of the skin containing pus) would burst and could expose such deep infection that a person's bones might be seen. Sometimes the infection completely ate away the eyes or lips. Later, swelling appeared, accompanied by violent pains in the muscles, a feeling of fatigue, and emaciation. Clearly, Europeans found syphilis to be a highly contagious, deadly, and disgusting disease.

By placing the origins of this disease in America, Europeans tried to incorporate it into their society with as little trauma as possible. They found some comfort in believing that syphilis, as an evil, came from a foreign place—at first a nearby country (hence, the French, Spanish, English disease), and then better yet, from a distant and alien territory (America), inhabited by an "enemy." By attributing the origin of syphilis to Native Americans, then, Europeans were undoubtedly suggesting that the origins of the sickness (or evil), which was tied to sexual excess, was located as far from European civilization as possible—in the totally alien, and for them, heathen civilization of Native Americans. Moreover, the fact that the disease attacked its victims' sexual organs fit nicely with the Europeans' tendency to stereotype Native Americans as extremely lustful people. For example, Amerigo Vespucci, who provided Europeans with many of their earliest images of Native American life, wrote that Native Americans had as many wives as they desired and lived in promiscuity without regard to blood relations. Mothers lie with sons, he wrote, and brothers with sisters. Oviedo gave a similar account that frequently emphasized the libidinous habits of the women in the Americas. He certainly had no doubts about the origin of syphilis and thought it should be called the "Indian disease."

Just as modern historians have debated the question of the origins of syphilis, they also disagree about its impact on European society. Again, sixteenth-century Europeans shared no such disagreement. Written evidence as well as paintings from the late fifteenth and early sixteenth centuries conclusively demonstrate their conviction that the disease was devastating the population. For example, in 1496 the French government ordered "pox-sufferers" to leave Paris until they healed—or be hanged. By the middle of the sixteenth century, authorities estimated that about a third of the population of Paris had become infected. Erasmus wrote that any nobleman who did not get syphilis was considered socially inept. In England in 1529, Sir Thomas More wrote that there were five times as many people suffering from syphilis in that year as in 1499, and in 1579 William Clowes, a London surgeon, wrote that about 75 percent of the patients admitted to St. Bartholomew's hospital suffered from syphilis. Syphilis, clearly, afflicted millions of ordinary Europeans, including several from the ruling class. It killed kings Charles VIII and Francis I of France, Pope Alexander VI (Rodrigo Borgia) and his nephew Pedro Borgia, and the Florentine artist Benvenuto Cellini. It may also have taken the lives of the English king Henry VIII and at least one (possibly two) of the husbands of Mary, Queen of Scots. Ulrich von Hutten, a German writer who died of syphilis in 1524, has left a detailed description of his suffering and his unsuccessful search for a cure:

> the saddest thing is that those who treated us in this fashion have themselves got no medical expertise. I have seen one healer cause three unfortunate artisans to perish in a steamroom whose temperature was raised on his recommendation. These patients, convinced that their cure would be quicker and more certain the higher the temperature they could bear, were stifled quite unaware of the nature of their unhappy end. I have seen others, whose swollen throats no longer allowed them to spit out or vomit up the purulent mucus, struggle in the grip of a most appalling agony and be suffocated by the corrupt fluids.[4]

On the other hand, however miserable syphilis may have been for the large number of its individual victims, some modern historians downplay its impact on Renaissance society as a whole. For one thing, they point out that the disease did not spread

---

4 Cited in Claude Quétel, *History of Syphilis* (Cambridge, UK: The Polity Press, 1990), 29.

quickly at the end of the fifteenth century. Even if we take 1493 as the correct date of the first appearance of a syphilis-like disease in Europe, about three years elapsed before it appeared in England. It appeared in Poland in 1499, and in Russia and Scandinavia only in 1500. It is also true that the European population continued to increase throughout the sixteenth century, when the disease was at its height. Indeed, some segments of the population no doubt benefitted from the opportunities that the deaths of others created. The wealthy Fugger family of German bankers, for example, added to the family fortune by becoming Europe's chief importers of guaiacum.

Possibly syphilis affected European social behavior more than any area of life. People stopped using common drinking cups, going to public bath houses, and kissing each other as a sign of friendship. At least one historian has even speculated that the degree of hospitality shown by Europeans to strangers or the sick may have also declined and that lovers became more careful in their relationships. The Italian author Gabriello Falloppio, for example, advised men in 1564 to carefully wash and dry their genitals after having sexual intercourse. Perhaps Erasmus summarized the effect of syphilis on the European lifestyle best in a dialogue he wrote between two characters named Petronious and Gabriel:

> P: At least so deadly a disease as this should have been treated with the same care as leprosy. But if this is too much to ask, no one should let his beard be cut, or else everybody should act as his own barber.
> G: What if everyone kept his mouth shut?
> P: They'd spread the disease through the nose.
> G: There's a remedy for that trouble too.
> P: What is it?
> G: Let them imitate the alchemists: wear a mask that admits light through glass windows and allows breath through mouth and nose by means of a tube extending from the mask over your shoulders and down your back.[5]

The exploration and conquest of America brought Europeans into contact with new foods, plants, animals, and medicinal

---

5 Cited in Alfred W. Crosby, Jr., *The Columbian Exchange. Biological and Cultural Consequences of 1492* (Westport, CT: The Greenwood Press, 1972), 160.

drugs. Together, these products probably enriched European civilization, especially in the long run, far more than all the gold and silver which attracted so much more attention at the time. Moreover, the uneven reception of these products, together with the frequent misunderstandings about their usefulness, helps shed light on the European mentality as it struggled to comprehend the "New World" that it had accidentally encountered. Sixteenth-century Europeans also came to believe that Native Americans had given them syphilis. The assumptions that they made about the origins and character of this malady are significant as well, because they illustrate not only some of the prevailing attitudes towards sickness and health in the Renaissance, but also the association that Europeans made between the existence of evil (in this case a sickness) and foreigners.

AFTERWORD

Readers may draw at least three conclusions from the material presented in this book. First, European civilization changed in some significant ways because of its relationship with America. At one level, these changes are easy to document. American gold and silver revitalized Europe's economy and brought forth new types of business organizations. Gradually, the centers of financial power began to shift from the Mediterranean to the Atlantic. At the same time, European governments extended their influence to the American continents, expanded their control to vast new lands, and fought against their rivals in these new arenas. European intellectuals pondered the meaning and implications of the Native American populations, and found themselves forced to reconsider some of their most cherished notions about their proper place among the peoples of the world.

At another level, it is not so easy to draw a close relationship between the "discovery" of America and the changes that took place in Renaissance Europe. In some cases, the American influence may well have been a decisive factor in bringing change, but in other areas—the so-called Price Revolution, for example—American influences may have only served to escalate the process of change.

Second, it appears obvious that Europeans living at the time of the "great discoveries" came to different conclusions about what happened to their civilization than do modern historians. This does not mean that they were wrong—only that they had a different outlook. From one point of view, people living through a great series of events experience them with an immediacy that no historian, studying the issues from afar, can hope to experience. On the other hand, however, later historians have the opportunity to observe events with a greater sense of perspective. They can understand the long-range consequences of trends and broad societal movements in ways that no one alive at the time could possibly hope to match. Even in those cases where it appears that sixteenth-century people were simply dead-wrong in their judgments about the causes of great events, their views are still important because they allow us to better understand the mentality of the age. On the other hand, even today, historians do not always agree in their interpretations of the past. Indeed, some historical problems, such as the origin of syphilis, have baffled scholars for a long time, and we may never have a definitive answer that is acceptable to everyone.

Third, the material in this book shows that events sometimes can have unexpected consequences. When Columbus set out in 1492, he wanted to pioneer a more efficient route to the riches of Asia. He never intended that any of the things described in this book should happen—he certainly did not hope to find a "New World." Historians sometimes speak of the "law of unintended consequences." What happened to European civilization in the period after 1492 is an excellent example of that law. These events demonstrate that no one can predict the direction or consequences of change. That makes predicting the future very difficult and the study of history extremely interesting.

BIBLIOGRAPHICAL ESSAY

Anyone who wants to learn more about the impact that the discovery of America had on European civilization should begin by consulting several key reference works and compilations of source materials. The most comprehensive among these are John Alden and Dennis Landis, *European Americana: A Chronological Guide to Works Printed in Europe Relating to the Americas, 1493–1776*, 4 vols. (New York: Readex Books, 1980–1988), which lists books published about America year-by-year starting in 1493. Although the individual entries are brief, the work provides an excellent summary of the literature on America. Dennis Landis has also published *The Literature of the Encounter: A Selection of Books from European Americana* (Providence, RI: The John Carter Brown Library, 1991). Here Landis focuses on sixty-one books that represented the kinds of writing that resulted from the interaction of Europeans and Native Americans in the first 250 years after Columbus's first voyage. Yet another guide to the literature of the encounter is *Keys to the Encounter: A Library of Congress Resource Guide for the Study of the Age of Discovery* (Washington, DC: Library of Congress, 1992), edited by Louis de Vorsey, Jr.

Two very useful compilations include both primary sources and more recent commentaries and interpretations. The better of these is Marvin Lunenfeld, *1492: Discovery, Invasion, Encounter: Sources and Interpretations* (Lexington, MA, and Toronto: D.C. Heath and Co., 1991). In addition to written accounts of the encounter between Native Americans and Europeans, Lunenfeld's work includes two sets of "picture portfolios," with commentaries. Dan O'Sullivan, *The Age of Discovery, 1400–1550* (London and New York: Longman, 1984), provides a similar compilation of sources and interpretations. Two other recent works present a selection of modern interpretations: Stuart B. Schwartz, *Implicit Understandings: Observing, Reporting, and Reflecting on the Encounters Between Europeans and Other Peoples in the Early Modern Era* (Cambridge and New York:

Cambridge University Press, 1994); and Karen O. Kupperman, ed., *America in European Consciousness, 1493–1750* (Chapel Hill and London: University of North Carolina Press, 1995). Finally, a special issue of the *William and Mary Quarterly*, 49 (April, 1992), edited by Michael McGiffert and entitled "Columbian Encounters," contains a series of articles on diverse political and cultural aspects of the meeting of Europeans and Native Americans.

Two books on the effect of America on Europe deserve special mention: J. H. Elliott, *The Old World and the New, 1492–1650* (Cambridge and New York: Cambridge University Press, 1970, reprinted 1983), and *First Images of America: The Impact of the New World on the Old*, edited by Fredi Chiappelli (Berkeley and Los Angeles: University of California Press, 1976). Based on a series of lectures given at Queen's University in Belfast, Elliott's thin volume—scarcely more than a hundred pages—is the first important book published on this subject. Although it appeared over twenty years ago, Elliott's work has remained valuable for its broad interpretations of the ways in which the discovery of America affected various spheres of European life. He examines the ways in which the discovery and conquest of America challenged traditional European assumptions about geography, theology, history, and human nature. Elliott also evaluates the extent to which American gold and silver stimulated economic and social change within Europe and how the Spanish conquest of America changed European political life.

Chiappelli's *First Images* reflects the influence of Elliott's pioneering work. This two-volume work, based on an international conference held at the University of California at Los Angeles in 1975, contains forty-three essays by distinguished scholars, covering virtually all aspects of the subject. While any attempt even to summarize the contents of these essays would result in an essay almost as long as this book, the following list of the most important articles will serve to illustrate the scope and significance of Chiappelli's edition. For discussions of the relationship between the main characteristics of Renaissance society and the Age of Exploration, see Charles Trinkaus, "Renaissance and Discovery":3–9; John H. Elliott, "Renaissance Europe and America: A Blunted Impact?":11–23; and Thomas Goldstein, "Impulses of Italian Renaissance Culture behind the

Age of Discoveries":27–35. Antonello Gerbi, "The Earliest Accounts of the New World":37–43; Wayland D. Hand, "The Effect of the Discovery on Ethnological and Folklore Studies in Europe":45–55; and Benjamin Keen, "The Vision of America in the Writings of Urbain Chauveton":107–20, provide useful studies of the initial European perceptions of America.

Some of the political ramifications of Europe's discovery of America are covered in Miguel Batllori, "The Papal Division of the World and Its Consequences":211–20; Charles H. Carter, "The New World as a Factor in International Relations, 1492–1739":231–63; and Geoffrey W. Symcox, "The Battle of the Atlantic, 1500–1700":265–77. For studies of the effect of America on the development of European theology see Wilcomb E. Washburn, "The Clash of Morality in the American Forest":335–50 and Lewis Hanke, "The Theological Significance of the Discovery of America":363–89. The image of America in European art, history, and language provides the focus for William C. Sturtevant, "First Visual Images of Native America":417–54; Suzanne Boorsch, "America in Festival Presentations":503–15; Myron P. Gilmore, "The New World in French and English Historians of the Sixteenth Century":519–27; and Stephen J. Greenblatt, "Learning to Curse: Aspects of Linguistic Colonialism in the Sixteenth Century":561–80.

The impact of America on the development of European geography is covered by three key articles: Hildegard Binder Johnson, "New Geographical Horizons: Concepts":615–33; David B. Quinn, "New Geographical Horizons: Literature":635–58; and Norman J. W. Thrower, "New Geographical Horizons: Maps":659–74. On the migrations of Europeans to America see Woodrow Borah, "The Mixing of Populations":707–22 and James Lockhart, "Letters and People to Spain":783–96. Finally, Joseph Ewan explores the American influence on European science and trade in "The Columbian Discoveries and the Growth of Botanical Ideas with Special Reference to the Sixteenth Century":807–12; Jonathan D. Sauer, "Changing Perception and Exploitation of New World Plants in Europe, 1492–1800":813–32; Charles H. Talbot, "America and the European Drug Trade":833–44; Francisco Guerra, "The Problem of Syphilis":845–51; and Earl J. Hamilton, "What the New World Gave the Economy of the

Old":853–84. For the period up to 1976, this impressive compilation certainly provides the most accurate and authoritative information about the various ways in which the discovery of America affected European civilization. The rest of this essay, therefore, will concentrate on books and articles published since the 1970s and written in English.

Most of the literature on the consequences of the Age of Exploration has focused on the effect that the European conquest had on American peoples and civilizations. This is not surprising because the European impact on America has had great historical significance. The effects—particularly the immediate impact—of America on Europe, on the other hand, appear relatively inconsequential by comparison. Columbus, after all, expected to find a new route to Asia rather than a "New World"—one that lacked the fabled wealth that Europeans hoped to find.

Perhaps the single most important book published on the American impact on European—and world—civilization is Alfred W. Crosby, *The Columbian Exchange: Biological and Cultural Consequences of 1492* (Westport, CT: Greenwood Press, 1972). By examining the interaction between the American and European ecosystems, Crosby permanently changed the way scholars have interpreted the historical significance of Columbus's "discovery" of America and brought the phrase "Columbian exchange" into common usage. In so doing, he made a strong case that the most important consequences of the contact between Europe and America were biological. Crosby discusses the role of smallpox in the Europeans' conquest and exploitation of the Native Americans, the importance of European plants in America, the history of syphilis, and the influence of American foods such as maize on the European population. In 1986 Crosby continued his pioneering work in *Ecological Imperialism: The Biological Expansion of Europe, 900–1900* (Cambridge and New York: Cambridge University Press, 1986). Here he broadened and refined the main themes of his earlier work on the transmission of diseases, animals, and plants from Europe to America and from America to other parts of the world. Crosby has also provided a good summary of the main points of his work in *The Columbian Voyages, the Columbian Exchange, and Their Historians*, a short pamphlet published by the American Historical Association in its series "Essays on Global and Comparative History" (Washington, DC: The American Historical Association, 1987).

Since the publication of Crosby's books, other historians have investigated further the themes which he had developed. The distinguished historian William McNeill, for example, published his own work, *Plagues and Peoples* (New York: Anchor Press, 1976), on the global interchange of diseases throughout history some four years after Crosby's *Columbian Exchange*. In this far-reaching discussion of the global exchange of diseases and their effect on the course of history, McNeill included a chapter on "Transoceanic Exchanges, 1500–1700," where he examines the history of syphilis and the Native Americans' vulnerability to such European diseases as smallpox and malaria. A more recent important work on syphilis, and especially on the relationship between how Europeans reacted to the disease and to the existence of Native Americans generally is Anna Foa, "The New and the Old: The Spread of Syphilis (1494–1530)," translated by Carole C. Gallucci, in *Sex and Gender in Historical Perspective*, edited by Edward Muir and Guido Ruggiero (Baltimore and London: The Johns Hopkins University Press, 1990):26–45. For more information on syphilis, see Claude Quetel, *The History of Syphilis*, translated by Judith Braddock and Brian Pike (Baltimore: Johns Hopkins University Press, 1992).

Crosby also influenced several studies of the movement of various foodstuffs and plants from one civilization to another. The first notable work to appear on this significant—but hitherto neglected subject—was Reay Tannahill, *Food in History* (New York: Stein and Day, 1973), which includes a chapter on "The Expanding World, 1490–1800." Raymond Sokolov's more recent *Why We Eat What We Eat: How the Encounter Between the New World and the Old Changed the Way Everyone on the Planet Eats* (New York: Summit Books, 1991), includes a more detailed, and entertaining, analysis of the same subject, especially in Part 3: "The New World Reshapes the Old." For the transmission of various plants from one part of the world to another, see Henry Hobhouse, *Seeds of Change: Five Plants that Transformed Mankind* (New York: Harper and Row, 1986). It focuses on the historical uses and benefits of quinine, sugar, tea, cotton, and the potato over the course of centuries. Three of these five "seeds" (quinine, sugar, and the potato) originated in the "Columbian Exchange." Another book called *Seeds of Change: A Quincentennial Commemoration*, edited by Herman J. Viola and Carolyn Margolis (Washington, DC: Smithsonian Institution Press, 1991) provides a lavishly illustrated companion to the museum exhibit of the same name. Containing fifteen articles written by experts in the field, it examines the long-range effects of livestock and agricultural exchanges after 1492, and also emphasizes five key catalysts (sugar, maize, disease, the horse, and the worldwide social revolution) stimulated by the encounter.

In recent years, scholars have published several books examining the impact that the discovery of Native Americans had on the European mentality. These books generally fall into two categories. The first of these focus mostly on the ways in which Europeans, or any group of people, perceive and assimilate foreigners, or what a number of authors refer to as "the Other." J. H. Elliott discusses this concept in the second chapter of *The Old World the New* ("The Process of Assimilation"), and he examines the impact of America on Renaissance thought more generally in "The Discovery of America and the Discovery of Man," which is chapter three in his collection of essays entitled *Spain and Its World, 1500–1700* (New Haven and London: Yale University Press, 1989). In the last decade or so, several crucial works on this theme have appeared, written primarily by critics of literature rather than by historians. One of the most important is Tzvetan Todorov, *The Conquest of America: The Question of the Other*. Originally written in French in 1982, Harper and Row published an English translation by Richard Howard in 1984. Todorov examines the conflicting beliefs of both the Aztecs and the Spaniards to ascertain how Europeans and Native Americans perceived each other. Although Todorov's book is intellectually stimulating, readers without some knowledge of literary theory may find it difficult. Equally provocative is Stephen Greenblatt, *Marvelous Possessions: The Wonder of the New World* (Chicago: University of Chicago Press, 1991). Through his analysis of various accounts of previously unknown peoples by Columbus and other explorers, Greenblatt sheds light on how Europeans represented non-European peoples, and how their "wonder" at the "New World" aroused in Europeans a desire to possess it. Another work with a similar theme is Peter Mason, *The Deconstructing of America: Representations of the Other* (New York: Routledge, 1990). Mason argues that even before Europeans "discovered" America, it already had a place in their collective imagination, and that these preconceived notions helped shape the ways in which Europeans reacted to the realities of the new American world. Mary B. Campbell provides yet another examination of European perceptions of "the Other" in *The Witness and the Other World: Exotic European Travel Writing, 400–1600* (Ithaca, NY, and London: Cornell University Press, 1988). This wide-ranging study includes samples of travel literature from a number of different historical periods. For the Age of Exploration, she examines the works of Columbus, Bartolomé de Las Casas, Walter Raleigh, and Alvar Núñez Cabeza de Vaca.

Historians and anthropologists was well as literary critics also have turned their attention to analyzing the ways in which the encounter between Europeans and Native Americans changed European perceptions of the world and of themselves. The connection between the European encounter with Native Americans and the development of modern anthropology is treated in Margaret T. Hodgen's classic *Early Anthropology in the Sixteenth and Seventeenth Centuries* (Philadelphia: University of Pennsylvania Press, 1964) and John H. Rowe, "Ethnography and Ethnology in the Sixteenth Century," *Kroeber Anthropological Society Papers* 30 (1964):1–19. In *The Fall of Natural Man: The American Indian and the Origins of Comparative Ethnology* (Cambridge and New York: Cambridge University Press, 1982), the British historian Anthony Pagden examines the various ways in which European thinkers tried to describe Native Americans and their societies and how those descriptions influenced the development of comparative ethnology. In his more recent *European Encounters with the New World* (New Haven and London: Yale University Press, 1993), Pagden extended his study of how European intellectuals used the concept of the "Noble Savage" to offer critiques of their own society from the Renaissance up to the Enlightenment. His work supersedes the earlier studies by Henri Baudet, *Paradise on Earth: Some Thoughts on European Images of Non-European Man*, translated by Elizabeth Wenthold

(New Haven and London: Yale University Press, 1965); Richard G. Cole, "Sixteenth-Century Travel Books as a Source of European Attitudes Toward Non-White and Non-Western Cultures," *Proceedings of the American Philosophical Society* 116 (1972):59–67; and Robert J. Berkhofer, Jr., *The White Man's Indian: Images of the American Indian from Columbus to the Present* (New York: Random House, 1979). An older study, still worth reading, is Carl O. Sauer, *Sixteenth-Century North America: The Land and the People as Seen by the Europeans* (Berkeley and Los Angeles: University of California Press, 1971). Good summaries of the major trends in recent scholarship in this area can be found in Dario Fernández-Morera, ed., "Europe and Its Encounter with the Amerindians," a special issue of the journal *History of European Ideas* 6 (1985) containing essays on Spanish and French interpretations of Native American cultures by experts in the subject. James Axtell, one of the leading authorities in American colonial history, has also reflected on the ways that Europeans and Native Americans envisioned one another in *Imagining the Other: First Encounters in North America* (Washington, DC: American Historical Association, 1991). An older, but still valuable study, is Wilcomb E. Washburn, "The Meaning of `Discovery' in the Fifteenth and Sixteenth Centuries," *The American Historical Review* 68 (1962):1–21.

Historians have also investigated the ways in which particular individuals came to grips with the concept of "New World." Columbus, of course, has received a good deal of attention, especially as a result of the recent quincentennial anniversary of his 1492 voyage. Four good recent books on Columbus are Felipe Fernández-Armesto, *Columbus* (Oxford and New York: Oxford University Press, 1991), a scholarly, well-documented biography of the famous explorer; Oliver Dunn and James E. Kelley, trans., *The Diario of Christopher Columbus' First Voyage to America, 1492–1493* (Norman: University of Oklahoma Press, 1989), the best translation of Bartolomé de Las Casas's abstract of Columbus's diary; Carla Rahn Phillips and William D. Phillips, *The Worlds of Christopher Columbus* (Cambridge and New York: Cambridge University Press, 1992), which places Columbus and his enterprise within the broader context of European history; and Valerie I. J. Flint, *The Imaginative Landscape of Christopher*

Columbus (Princeton: Princeton University Press, 1992), a careful examination of Columbus's perceptions of America. Anthony Pagden, *Hernán Cortés: Letters from Mexico* (New Haven and London: Yale University Press, 1986), provides good translations of Cortés's impressions of Aztec civilization, and includes a thorough set of notes to help explain the importance of the text. Benjamin Keen, *The Aztec Image in Western Thought* (New Brunswick, NJ: Rutgers University Press, 1971; reprinted 1985) also examines how Europeans interpreted Aztec civilization, and shows how these various interpretations are related to the social, political, and intellectual climate of the time. The Spanish encounter with Native Americans is also the subject of Urs Bitterli, *Cultures in Conflict: Encounters between European and Non-European Cultures, 1492–1800* (Stanford: Stanford University Press, 1989), and Peter Hulme, *Colonial Encounters: Europe and the Native Caribbean, 1492–1797* (London and New York: Methuen, 1986). A good collection of essays on related themes is found in *Indians and Europe: An Interdisciplinary Collection of Essays,* edited by Christian F. Feest (Aachen, Germany: Editions Herodot, 1987). Bartolomé de Las Casas has been the subject of several studies that shed light on European perceptions of Native Americans. Among the more important are *Bartolomé de Las Casas in History,* edited by Juan Friede and Benjamin Keen (De Kalb, IL: Northern Illinois University Press, 1971), and Lewis Hanke, *All Mankind is One: A Study of the Disputation between Bartolomé de Las Casas and Juan Ginés de Sepúlveda in 1550 on the Intellectual and Religious Capacity of the American Indians* (De Kalb,IL: Northern Illinois University Press, 1974).

The reactions of the French to American peoples and society has been an especially important field of study in the last decade or so. The most significant work in this area has been by Cornelius J. Jaenen and Olive P. Dickason. Jaenen examines French attitudes towards Native Americans in *Friend and Foe: Aspects of French-Amerindian Cultural Contact in the Sixteenth and Seventeenth Centuries* (New York: Columbia University Press, 1976), and in some significant articles: "Conceptual Frameworks for French Views of America and Amerindians," *French Colonial Studies* 2 (1978):1–22, and "France's America and Amerindians: Image and Reality," *History of European Ideas* 6 (1985):405–52.

Dickason's most important work is *The Myth of the Savage and the Beginnings of French Colonialism in the Americas* (Edmonton: University of Alberta Press, 1984), but she has also written "The Concept of *l'homme sauvage* and early French colonialism in the Americas," *Revue française d'histoire d'outre-mer* 64 (1977):5–32, and "European and Amerindian: Some Comparative Aspects of Early Contact," Canadian Historian Association, *Historical Papers* (1979):182–202. Amy G. Gordon provides a case study of how European contact with America and its inhabitants changed historical thinking in "Confronting Cultures: The Effect of the Discoveries on Sixteenth-Century French Thought," *Terrae Incognitae* 8 (1976):45–56. Janet Whatley has translated Jean de Léry's important account of his experiences in Brazil, *History of a Voyage to the Land of Brazil, Otherwise Called America* (Berkeley and Los Angeles: University of California Press, 1990), while Roger Schlesinger and Arthur P. Stabler have made the work of André Thevet, a second sixteenth-century French traveler to the Americas, available in *André Thevet's North America: A Sixteenth-Century View* (Kingston and Montreal: McGill-Queen's University Press, 1986). Thevet's pioneering biographies of six Native Americans, including a copperplate engraving of each subject, are included in Roger Schlesinger and Edward Benson's edition of *Portraits from the Age of Exploration: Selections from André Thevet's Vrais Portraits et Vies des Hommes Illustres* (Urbana and Chicago: University of Illinois Press, 1993).

There are several books that examine how the European encounter with Native Americans influenced certain areas of European intellectual or cultural life. One of the most interesting is William Brandon, *New Worlds for Old: Reports from the New World and their Effect on the Development of Social Thought in Europe, 1500–1800* (Athens, OH: Ohio University Press, 1986), which asserts that European contact with American civilizations resulted in profound, even revolutionary, change in European social thought. Another stimulating work is J.-P. Rubiés, "Hugo Grotius's Dissertation on the Origin of the American Peoples and the Use of Comparative Methods," *Journal of the History of Ideas* 52 (1991):221–24. The ways in which European artists portrayed America and its inhabitants is assessed in Hugh Honour's illustrated survey, *The New Golden Land: European Images of America, From the Discoveries to the Present Time* (New York: Pantheon, 1975), and treated from a more narrow perspective in Bernadette Bucher, *Icon and Conquest: A Structural Analysis of the Illustrations of de Bry's Great Voyages*, translated by Basia Miller Gulati (Chicago: University of Chicago Press, 1981). Two of the most important artists to depict America were the Englishman John White and the Frenchman Jacques Le Moyne. Their work has been studied by Paul Hulton and David Beers Quinn, eds., *The American Drawings of John White, 1577–1590*, 2 vols. (London: British Museum Publications and University of North Carolina Press, 1964), and Paul Hulton, ed., *The Work of Jacques Le Moyne de Morgues: A Huguenot Artist in France, Florida, and England*, 2 vols. (London: British Museum Publications, in association with the Huguenot Society of London, 1977). Finally, Antonio Gerbi's classic account of changing European conceptions of the natural world, *Nature in the New World, From Christopher Columbus to Gonzalo Fernández de Oviedo*, translated by J. Moyle Pitts (Pittsburgh: University of Pittsburgh Press, 1985), contains an excellent discussion and analysis of the early explorers' impressions of the American scene.

The relative scarcity of recent books on the ways in which the European discovery of America influenced political or economic developments reflects the disinterest that many contemporary historians have for these traditional areas of investigation. One classic that deserves special mention is Roger B. Merriman, *The Rise of the Spanish Empire in the Old World and the New*, 4 vols. (New York: Macmillan, 1918–34). Older books that are still worth consulting include J. H. Parry, *The Spanish Seaborne Empire* (New York: Knopf, 1966) and, by the same author, *The Spanish Theory of Empire in the Sixteenth Century* (Cambridge and New York: Cambridge University Press, 1940). Among more recent studies, the more important are Anthony Pagden, *Spanish Imperialism and the Political Imagination* (New Haven and London: Yale University Press, 1990); Kenneth R. Andrews, *Trade, Plunder, and Settlement: Maritime Enterprise and the Genesis of the British Empire, 1480–1630* (Cambridge and New York: Cambridge University Press, 1984); Lyle N. McAlister, *Spain and Portugal in the New World, 1492–1700* (Minneapolis: University of Minnesota Press, 1984); and G. V. Scammell, *The World Encompassed: The First*

European Maritime Empires c. 800–1650 (Berkeley and Los Angeles: University of California Press, 1981), especially chapters six through nine, and by the same author, "The New Worlds and Europe in the Sixteenth Century, *The Historical Journal* 12 (1969):389–412. The relationship between European expansion and the development of international law is the subject of Olive P. Dickason, "Renaissance Europe's View of Amerindian Sovereignty and Territoriality," *Plural Societies* 8 (1977):97–107, and "Old World Law, New World Peoples, and Concepts of Sovereignty," in *Essays on the History of North American Discovery and Exploration*, edited by Stanley H. Palmer and Dennis Reinhartz (College Station, TX: University of Texas at Arlington [published by Texas A and M University Press], 1988):52–78; Anthony Pagden, "Dispossessing the Barbarian: the Language of Spanish Thomism and the Debate Over the Property Rights of the American Indians," in *The Languages of Political Theory in Early-Modern Europe*, edited by Anthony Pagden (Cambridge and New York: Cambridge University Press, 1987):79–98; and Richard Tuck, "The 'Modern' Theory of Natural Law," Ibid.:99–119. Paul E. Hoffman, *A New Andalucía and a Way to the Orient* (Baton Rouge: Louisiana State University Press, 1990) explores the rivalries among the Spaniards, French, and English in Florida and neighboring areas.

The key book on the influence of America on European economic developments is Earl J. Hamilton's classic study, *American Treasure and the Price Revolution in Spain, 1501–1650* (New York: Octagon Books, 1965). Two older books that still merit consideration are Clarence H. Haring, *Trade and Navigation between Spain and the Indies in the Time of the Hapsburgs* (Gloucester, MA: Peter Smith publisher, 1964), and Ruth Pike, *Enterprise and Adventure: The Genoese in Seville and the Opening of the New World* (Ithaca, NY: Cornell University Press, 1966). More general studies include Walter Prescott Webb's classic, *The Great Frontier* (Boston: Houghton-Mifflin, 1952), which applies the "frontier thesis" of the American West to European expansion, and Ralph E. Davis, *The Rise of the Atlantic Economies* (Ithaca, NY: Cornell University Press, 1973). Philip D. Curtin uses a broader approach to the question of America's role in European, and worldwide economic developments in, *Cross-Cultural Trade in World History*

(Cambridge and New York: Cambridge University Press, 1984), and Immanuel Wallerstein, *The Modern World-System,* vol. 1 (New York: Academic Press, Inc., 1974) offers a controversial approach to the subject.

Finally, a good overview of America's impact on European civilization can be gleaned from Carlo Cipolla, *European Culture and Overseas Expansion* (Harmondsworth, UK: Penguin Books, 1970); M. T. Ryan, "Assimilating New Worlds in the Sixteenth and Seventeenth Centuries," *Comparative Studies in Society and History* 23 (1981):519–38; Germán Arciniegas, *America in Europe: A History of the New World in Reverse,* translated by Gabriela Arciniegas and R. Victoria Arana (New York: Harcourt Brace Jovanovich, 1986); and Anthony Grafton, *New Worlds, Ancient Texts: The Power of Tradition and the Shock of Discovery* (Cambridge, MA: Harvard University Press, 1992). Since this bibliographical essay began with a consideration of one of J. H. Elliott's books, it is fitting that we conclude with the same author's "The World After Columbus," *The New York Review of Books* 38 (October 10, 1991):10–14.

INDEX

In the Wake of Columbus: The Impact of the New World on Europe, 1492–1650

Sponsoring editor and copy editor, Maureen Hewitt
Production editor, Lucy Herz
Proofreader, Claudia Siler
Typesetter, Bruce Leckie
Printer, Thomson-Shore, Inc.

About the Author: Roger Schlesinger is Chair of the History Department and Professor of History at Washington State University. He is author of *André Thevet's North America: A Sixteenth-Century View* (1986) and *Portraits from the Age of Exploration* (1993), and is recipient of the Burlington Northern Award for Faculty Achievement.